From Garden to Table

GROWING & ARRANGING
FLOWERS

From Garden to Table

GROWING & ARRANGING FLOWERS

Pamela Thomas

CRESCENT BOOKS
New York

A FRIEDMAN GROUP BOOK

This 1991 edition published by Crescent Books,
distributed by Outlet Book Company, Inc., a Random House Company
225 Park Avenue South
New York, New York 10003

ISBN 0-517-03747-5

FROM GARDEN TO TABLE
GROWING AND ARRANGING FLOWERS
was prepared and produced by
Michael Friedman Publishing Group, Inc.
15 West 26th Street
New York, New York 10010

Editor: Melissa Schwarz
Art Director: Jeff Batzli
Designer: Lynne Yeamans
Photo Researcher: Anne K. Price
Illustrator: Anne L. Meskey

Typeset by The Interface Group, Inc.
Color separation by Excel Graphic Arts Co.
Printed and bound in Hong Kong by LeeFung-Asco Printers Limited

8 7 6 5 4 3 2 1

DEDICATION

To my mother
Roberta Bosworth Mathews

ACKNOWLEDGMENTS

Several people helped to bring this book to flower. At the Michael Friedman Group, I would like to thank Karla Olson, Sharyn Rosart, Jeff Batzli, Lynne Yeamans, and especially Melissa Schwarz.

I want to thank Jerry Rose, the artist and florist who created the "gallery" of arrangements that appear in this book. Jerry not only applied his talented eye to the flowers, he added his humor, his hard work, and his patience to make this book special. I also appreciate the cooperation and intelligent participation of Jerry's aide, Pam Fani.

Finally, I would like to thank Jon, Nina, Julia, and Sophia Day for permitting me to invade their lives and use the basics of their lovely garden in this book.

The publisher would like to thank Katalin and Fred Potter and Betty and Richard Saccaro for generously allowing their lovely homes to be photographed.

© Derek Fell

© Charles Mann

Contents

—

INTRODUCTION

© Derek Fell

Writing a relatively short but useful book about flowers—especially one with the theme "flowers, from garden to table"—is a challenge. I have tried to cover both growing flowers in the garden—a virtually infinite subject; cultivating flowers indoors—a topic almost as endless as its outdoor counterpart; and to offer a good, basic introduction to arranging fresh and dried flowers. The result is a book that I hope will give beginning gardeners a solid base from which to explore these rich and fascinating subjects.

9

Opposite: Pansies add a rainbow of color to spring borders.

Any form of gardening requires careful planning and imagination, and flower gardening, in some ways, demands the most thought of all. A classic herb garden or an ambitious vegetable patch is meant to be harvested. The fruits of the garden are intended to be pulled up the moment they are ripe and, therefore, plans for designing and cultivating the garden can be made relatively simply.

Flowers, on the other hand, are grown for the pleasure of their color, fragrance, and beauty, and are meant to serve as both decoration and enhancement in the yard and inside the home. Most flowers bloom for only a short period of time. Daffodils and crocuses welcome us to spring, then die back; chrysanthemums bloom at the end of summer and remain for a few weeks into the fall. Therefore, a flowering border or flower bed must be organized so that it boasts blooms throughout the growing season.

For those who plan to cut back their flowers and greens at the very moment they are at their most beautiful, the task of creating an attractive flower garden becomes a bit more complicated. First, the gardener must plan for a garden that blooms continuously, but also produces flowers (and foliage) that will work well in arrangements. These plans must take into consideration color, style, fragrance—both in the garden and in arrangements. In addition, thought must be given to having certain flowers bloom simultaneously. Further, the gardener must plan the garden in such a way that the garden itself remains attractive even after the beautiful blooms have been picked.

However, this sounds far more complicated than it actually is. Gardeners have thousands of flowers and plants to choose from, and finding those that work for your climate, your personal landscape, and your taste is always part of the fun of gardening, rather than a chore.

Bringing beautiful, fragrant flowers into the house and placing them in every nook and cranny is a great part of the delight of flower gardening. Knowing the basics of flower arranging, including both creating the arrangements and maintaining the life of the flowers themselves, is essential. Knowing how to dry flowers and foliage for "everlasting" arrangements can add even greater enjoyment to the "fruits" of the flower garden.

Thus, in this book, I have provided a beginner's guide to cultivating a flower garden, combined with directions for gathering those flowers and creating exciting arrangements indoors. Part of the joy of gardening is that a gardener is constantly learning. The information available about flowers and how they can be cultivated and used is boundless. However, it is my hope that this book will provide the essential information that will allow you to begin to take part in the never-ending pleasure of gardening with flowers.

— *Part I* —

© Derek Fell

THE FLOWER ARRANGER'S GARDEN

Chapter 1

—

FACTS ABOUT FLOWERS

Foxglove, an old-fashioned English country garden flower, is enjoying new popularity.

Before you can begin to plan any flower garden, it is necessary to know a bit about flowers and other flowering plants, and the various ways they can be added productively and attractively to your landscape. In general terms, flowers (as well as most other plants) are categorized as: annuals, biennials, perennials, and bulbs.

14

Annuals are plants that grow, flower, set seed, and die in one growing season. Biennials are plants that require two or three seasons to complete their growing cycle, while perennials bloom in spring or summer, die back in the fall, remain dormant throughout the winter, and bloom again in spring. Perennials (and, to some extent, biennials) are also evaluated in relation to their ability to survive in particular "zones," and since they remain in the earth year after year, their hardiness must be considered carefully. In fact, some delicate biennials and perennials are grown more successfully as annuals—at least in some regions, climates, or zones.

When flowers are referred to as "perennials," gardeners are talking about herbaceous flowering plants, such as the common aster, baby's-breath, or various chrysanthemums. Technically, however, trees, shrubs, bushes, and bulbs are also perennials since they bloom repeatedly year after year. Certain flowering trees and shrubs such as cherry trees, dogwood trees, lilac bushes, or forsythia should be considered for any garden for all the reasons certain flowers are grown: They are beautiful, often fragrant, and their flowering boughs add to indoor arrangements. Evergreen shrubs and trees are also imperative in a landscape, and should be included. Of course, the "bush" most commonly evoked in the garden is the "rose bush"—and roses are the most popular flower in the world.

Bulbs are also a special case. Bulbs, of course, are among the most beautiful and popular flowers in the flower arranger's garden. Daffodils, tulips, and lilies are just a few of the flowers grown from bulbs. In fact, bulbs are not difficult to cultivate, but they do require special attention—depending upon the climate. Although they will continue to bloom for many years, in some situations they may need to be brought indoors during the colder months.

Given all the choices—annuals, perennials, bulbs, trees, and shrubs—a flower garden can be planned in a multitude of ways. A "cutting garden" of annuals may be planted in one area of the yard, while a border or borders of perennial flowers adorn other areas. A rock garden or decorative bed containing an assortment of annuals, perennials, and bulbs may be designed to create a focal point on the landscape. Or, a bed of spring bulbs may be positioned in a particular plot, only to be followed, after the tulips or hyacinths have died back, by summer perennials in the same place. Regardless of the choices—and they are infinite—the creativity is in the hands of the gardener.

ANNUALS

Many serious gardeners consider annuals to be gaudy—and fickle—usurpers on the garden landscape. Bright snapdragons, bluebells, marigolds, and zinnias are easy to grow, and unlike perennials, remain only for one season, so if a "mistake" is made in color or style, it isn't a serious loss. Nevertheless, annual flowers are some of the most colorful, and therefore among the most welcome in a flower arranger's garden. (See the list of "Annuals for Cutting" on page 17.)

Annuals (flowers as well as other annual plants) are categorized as "hardy," "half-hardy," and "tender," and these descriptions reflect the plant's relationship to the prevailing climate. Hardy annuals can tolerate frost and can be planted before the last frost—or will bloom year-round in warmer climates. Half-hardy annuals will tolerate cold, but will be killed by frost, while tender annuals require warmth, and must be planted after the last winter frost. As with all garden plants, choosing those annual flowers that will grow best in your garden depends upon your climate and the condition of your soil. Consult a good general flower book or a seed catalog that contains detailed flower descriptions in order to find the flowers that will suit the particular conditions of your garden site.

The Cutting Garden

The term "cutting garden" is a rather old-fashioned expression, and denotes an area or plot in the garden set aside especially for annual flowers that are intended to be "cut" for use indoors. A cutting garden can be cultivated in a casual way, with a few annual flowers incorporated into an herb or vegetable garden. Some seed companies sell "packages" or "kits" of "cutting garden flowers" which usually contain a hodgepodge of seeds that can be easily scattered in any prepared bed. With such kits, you won't know what flowers you have grown until they come up—which can be serendipitous for a creative gardener.

On the other hand, you may want to create a more formal or organized space, planting specific annual seeds and/or plants in a particular arrangement. Your choices will depend not only on your climate and soil, but also on your personal likes and dislikes with regard to garden design and your choice of flowers for arrangements. For example, you may wish to grow predominantly red flowers—such as zinnias, poppies, or asters—which would serve to add a bright spot of color in your garden and, when gathered and arranged, enhance the decor of your home.

In any case, a "cutting garden" of bright annuals is a necessity for the flower arranger's garden. By midsummer, whether you scattered seeds in a plot next to your vegetables or carefully planned and created a grid of bright flowers, you will delight in your crop. In addition, since many annual flowers dry easily and well, you may decide to preserve your flowers in order to enjoy them for many months after they have decorated your garden.

ANNUALS FOR CUTTING

The following is a list of some of the annual flowers that are popular for use in indoor arrangements:

Hollyhock	*Althaea rosea*
Snapdragon	*Antirrhinum majus*
African daisy	*Arctotis stoechadifolia*
Pot marigold	*Calendula officinalis*
China aster	*Callistephus chinensis*
Canterbury-bells	*Campanula medium*
Cockscomb	*Celosia cristata*
Centaurea	*Centaurea*
Bachelor's-button	*Centaurea cyanus*
Chrysanthemum	*Chrysanthemum*
Farewell-to-spring	*Clarkia amoena*
Spider flower	*Cleome spinosa*
Rocket larkspur	*Consolida ambigua*
Garden cosmos	*Cosmos astrosanguineus*
Dahlia	*Dahlia*
China pink	*Dianthus chinensis*
Foxglove	*Digitalis purpurea*
Cape marigold	*Dimorphotheca pluvialis*
California poppy	*Eschscholzia californica*
Prairie gentian	*Eustoma grandiflorum*
Blanketflower	*Gaillardia*
Gerbera	*Gerbera jamesonii*
Sunflower	*Helianthus annuus*
Rose mallow	*Hibiscus syriacus*

Top: The African daisy is one of the most dramatic and popular annuals. Bottom: Canterbury Bells is actually a biennial that is usually grown as an annual.

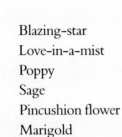

Blazing-star	*Liatris spicata*
Love-in-a-mist	*Nigella damascena*
Poppy	*Papaver*
Sage	*Salvia*
Pincushion flower	*Scabiosa astropurpurea*
Marigold	*Tagetes*
Blue laceflower	*Trachymene coerulea*
Zinnia	*Zinnia elegans*

Top: Annual poppies add color and drama to the garden. Bottom: Mexican sunflower can be a striking addition to the garden, and is an excellent flower for drying.

ANNUALS FOR DRYING

Ageratum	*Ageratum mexicanum*
Celosia	*Celosia plumosa*
Bachelor's button	*Centaurea cyanus*
Globe amaranth	*Gomphrenia globosa*
Baby's-breath	*Gypsophila paniculata*
Strawflower (Everlasting)	*Helichrysum bracteatum*
Statice	*Limonium sinuatum*
Lunaria	*Lunaria biennis*
Evening primrose	*Oenothera biennis*
Mexican sunflower	*Tithonia rotundifolio*
Zinnia	*Zinnia elegans*

PERENNIALS

Perennials are perhaps the most rewarding garden flower in that they bloom year after year and usually require only a minimum of care. And, because they have been planned carefully, they tend to create a stable and stylish look in a landscape.

Like all plants, the type of perennials you choose for your garden depends upon your climate in general, and particularly the "zone" in which you live. (See hardiness zone map, page 28.) Your choices also rest on the nature of your personal landscape, that is your "microclimate," which includes elements such as the presence of large trees, the extent of sun your property receives, and the size of your garden beds. Naturally, plant choices also reflect your personal preferences with regard to color, form, fragrance, and style.

The following list catalogs a number of perennial flowers that are particularly suited for cutting and arranging, but you should also consider including perennial plants in your garden that may serve only to decorate and enhance the garden itself. For example, columbine, boltonia, and golden flax are beautiful flowers that will definitely add color and fragrance to a garden, but may not necessarily be the best choices for creating indoor flower arrangements. Since they will not be harvested as readily, these flowers will allow a garden to remain full and lush. The variety of perennial flowers is virtually infinite, and both "cutting" flowers and "garden" flowers are necessary to ensure that the garden remains attractive all season long.

Top: Painted daisies are colorful, easy-to-grow perennials. Bottom: Delphiniums are attractive, both in the garden and in arrangements.

PERENNIALS FOR CUTTING

The following is a list of some of the perennial flowers and plants that are particularly suitable for cutting and arranging:

Bear's breeches   *Acanthus mollis*
Fern-leaf yarrow   *Achillea filipendulina*

Top: Purple coneflower is a nice addition to the perennial garden because it often blooms well into autumn. Bottom: Oriental poppies are classic perennials for late spring.

Common yarrow	*Achillea millefolium*
Golden marguerite	*Anthemis tinctoria*
Aster (many varieties)	*Aster*
Blue false indigo	*Baptisia australis*
Blue Cupid's dart	*Catananche caerulea*
Centaurea (many varieties)	*Centaurea*
Red valerian	*Centranthus ruber*
Pyrethrum	*Tanacetum coccineum*
Shasta daisy	*Chrysanthemum maximum*
Larkspur	*Consolida*
Coreopsis	*Coreopsis*
Delphinium	*Delphinium*
Pink	*Dianthus*
Purple cone flower	*Echinacea purpurea*
Fleabane	*Erigeron*
Sea holly	*Eryngium*
Euphorbia	*Euphorbia*
Blanketflower	*Gaillardia*
Avens	*Geum*
Baby's-breath	*Gypsophila*
Sneezeweed	*Helenium*
Perennial sunflower	*Helianthus* x *multiflorus*
Inula	*Inula*
Torch lily	*Kniphofia*
Peony	*Paeonia*
Oriental poppy	*Papaver orientale*
Dwarf balloon flower	*Platycodon grandiflorus*
Showy stonecrop	*Sedum spectabile*

PERENNIALS FOR DRYING

Fern-leaf yarrow	*Achillea filipendulina*
Common yarrow	*Achillea millefolium*
Pearly everlasting	*Anaphalis margaritacea*
Astilbe	*Astilbe japonica*
Blue false indigo	*Baptisia australis*
Globethistle	*Echinops humilis*
Baby's-breath	*Gypsophila elegans*
Perennial sunflower	*Helianthus* x *multiflorus*
Torch lily	*Kniphofia*
Lupin	*Lupinus polyphyllus*

The torch lily or poker plant is a particularly useful plant for drying.

GREENS FOR THE CUTTING GARDEN

Silver mound artemisia	*Artemisia schmidtiana*
Sweet grass	*Glyceria maxima*
Zebra grass	*Miscanthus sinensis*
Soapweed	*Yucca glauca*

Flowering Trees and Shrubs

Although they are not herbaceous perennials (and therefore not "true" perennials), certain flowering trees and bushes are considered an important part of most gardeners' landscapes. Lilac and forsythia are popular bushes, although neither is particularly attractive when its flowers are not in bloom. Certain trees such as dogwood and cherry bloom only briefly in the spring, but their short "period in the sun" is so spectacular that they are well worth cultivating.

In more temperate climates, citrus trees such as lemon, orange, and lime are also well worth the effort. The fragrance of orange blossoms, for example, is unequalled.

Planting and pruning trees usually requires the assistance of a professional. Ask at your local garden center for advice on planting flowering trees.

With regard to flower arrangements, the boughs and branches from flowering shrubs and trees make delightful additions, and can be used in unique and creative ways.

A Word About Roses

No garden designed for flower arranging would be complete without roses. In variety of shape, color—and, certainly, fragrance—no flower equals the rose. Unfortunately, roses are among the most difficult plants to grow since they are particularly prey to pests and disease and are finicky about their environment (soil, sunlight, and weather). Nevertheless, they are well worth the trouble. In a beginner's garden, plant two or three rose bushes in a small bed where they can be easily seen and appreciated. Ask at your garden center for the varieties that thrive in your region.

The ornamental peach is one of the loveliest of flowering trees.

© Derek Fell

22

FLOWERING TREES AND SHRUBS

The following is a list of suggested flowering shrubs and trees you might wish to consider for your garden:

Trees

Japanese maple	*Acer palmatum*
Birch	*Betula*
Dogwood	*Cornus*
Quince	*Cydonia*
Magnolia	*Magnolia*
Apple	*Malus*
Flowering crab	*Malus*
Cherry	*Prunus*
Peach	*Prunus*
Plum	*Prunus*

Shrubs

Boxwood	*Buxus*
Euonymous	*Euonymus fortunei*
Forsythia	*Forsythia*
Witch hazel	*Hamamelis*
Hydrangea	*Hydrangea macrophylla*
Heavenly bamboo	*Nanclina domestica*
Spirea	*Spirea*
Lilac	*Syringa*
Japanese yew	*Taxus cuspidata*

Top: Forsythia blooms beautifully in early spring, but is not a particularly attractive plant during the rest of the year. Bottom: Dogwood blooms only briefly, but its color and fragrance make it a marvelous addition to spring bouquets.

BULBS

Bulbs are usually associated with the vivid flowers of spring—daffodils, tulips, hyacinths, crocuses—but, in fact, some bulb plants—irises, begonias, and lilies—enliven a garden throughout the growing season.

The term "bulb" is often used loosely and includes flowers that are true bulbs as well as corms, tubers, tuberous roots, and rhizomes. Bulbs grow well in many climates, make beautiful formal borders and beds, and, as a result of their vivid color, add a rich, vivid quality to a relaxed country garden. Bulbs can also be easily grown in containers and window boxes, and even indoors to create a year-round flower garden.

Bulbs last for years, but in certain climates and conditions, they may need to be dug up and stored during periods of dormancy. Also, in some conditions, dormancy may need to be artificially enforced. For detailed instructions for selecting appropriate bulbs for your region and for cultivating bulbs, look for one of the many guides to growing bulbs. (See "Suggested Reading," page 125.)

Top: Dahlias are tender bulbs that bloom from late summer into autumn in most climates. Bottom: Gladiolus is another tender bulb that brings a wide range of soft hues to the summer garden. This variety, known as 'Peter Pears,' comes in an interesting shade of soft peach.

BULBS FOR CUTTING

Following is a list of some of the flowering plants grown from bulbs that are appropriate for floral arrangements:

African lily	*Agapanthus africanus*
Ornamental onion	*Allium*
Tuberous begonia	*Begonia* x *terhybrida*
Camas	*Camassia*
Glory-of-the-snow	*Chionodoxa*
Lily-of-the-valley	*Convallaria majalis*
Fumewort	*Corydalis bulbosa*
Dahlia	*Dahlia*
Winter aconite	*Eranthis*
Foxtail lily	*Eremurus*

Amazon lily	*Eucharis grandiflora*
Freesia	*Freesia*
Snowdrop	*Galanthus*
Gladiolus	*Gladiolus*
Gloxinia	*Sinningia speciosa*
Daylily	*Hemerocallis*
Bluebell	*Campanula rotundifolia*
Garden hyacinth	*Hyacinthus orientalis*
Iris	*Iris*
Corn lily	*Ixia*
Snowflake	*Leucojum*
Lily	*Lilium*
Grape hyacinth	*Muscari*
Daffodil or narcissus	*Narcissus*
Ranunculus	*Ranunculus asiaticus*
Lily-of-the-field	*Sternbergia lutea*
Trillium	*Trillium*
Tulip	*Tulipa*

© Charles Mann

Lilies come in infinite varieties and are among the most popular bulbs.

GREENS FROM BULBS

Fancy-leaved caladium	*Caladium* x *hortulanum*
Elephant-ear	*Kalanchoe beharensis*

Chapter 2

PLANNING THE GARDEN

© Charles Mann

Planning your garden is one of the most pleasurable aspects of gardening. Choosing the plants you wish to cultivate and their placement in your garden requires careful attention, both from a practical point of view and from an aesthetic or "design" perspective. The time and effort you take at this juncture in the gardening process will be well worth the investment.

Practical Considerations

The first step toward planning a flower garden is to carefully evaluate the site where your garden will grow with reference to the plants you wish to grow there. You must consider your climate (especially the prevailing temperatures), and the zone in which you live. (See Hardiness Zone Map, page 28.) Obviously, a gardener in Vancouver will have to plan his garden—and the timing of his planting—much differently than a gardener in south Florida. Most flowers mentioned in this book thrive in most parts of North America, but consult a complete gardening guide, your garden center, and various seed and plant catalogs for plants that may grow particularly well in your area. (For example, certain tropical flowers such as amaryllis, orchids, cyclamen, or jasmine—some of which are spectacularly beautiful—will grow best in warmer parts of the American South, and Southerners should not hesitate to add those flowers to their gardens.)

After giving general thought to your local climate, consider the amount of sunlight your particular garden receives. Of course, sunlight is of primary importance in a flower garden, and although sunlight requirements vary from flower to flower, most require five to six hours of sunlight per day. (For the individual needs of particular flowers, refer to a general garden guide.) At the same time, many plants require some shade—especially in warmer climates, where the sun can be intense during the warm hours of the day. The particular architectural details of your own landscape are also important. Before you plant, be sure that large trees, fences, or buildings will not be casting cool shadows over your flower beds during important sunlight hours.

The texture and richness of your soil as well as the drainage potential should also be considered very carefully. Most flower beds require some "soil preparation" to adjust the acidity, provide proper nutrients, and create a texture that allows for adequate drainage. (For detailed directions, see "Preparing the Soil," page 45.) Again, the care you take in preparing your flower beds will pay off in happy, lush flowers.

James Underwood Crockett, in his book *Crockett's Flower Garden*, suggests that the first step toward planning a garden is to find plants that suit the various spots you wish to cultivate, rather than trying to find spots in the garden to place your favorite plants. This may sound a bit backwards since for many of us our first thought is that we most definitely want a border of candytuft, for example; yet, when we research the situation, we may discover that the border area is not sunny enough to support this plant. As Mr. Crockett suggests, it is far easier to observe that we

USDA Plant Hardiness Zone Map

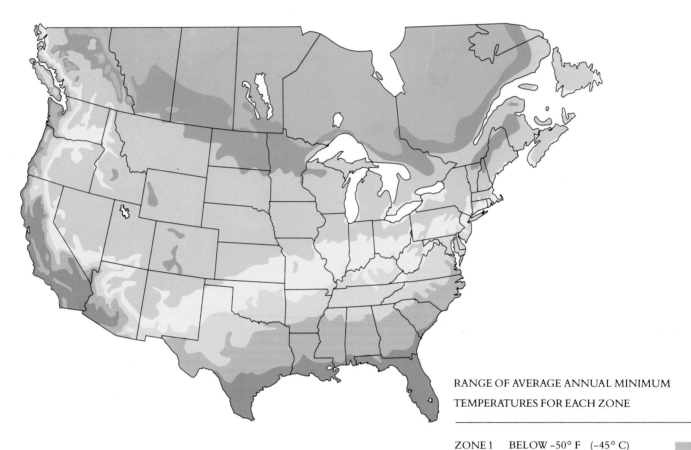

RANGE OF AVERAGE ANNUAL MINIMUM
TEMPERATURES FOR EACH ZONE

ZONE 1	BELOW –50° F	(–45° C)
ZONE 2	–50° TO –40°	(–45° to –40°)
ZONE 3	–40° TO –30°	(–40° to –34°)
ZONE 4	–30° TO –20°	(–34° to –28°)
ZONE 5	–20° TO –10°	(–28° to –23°)
ZONE 6	–10° TO 0°	(–23° to –17°)
ZONE 7	0° TO 10°	(–17° to –12°)
ZONE 8	10° TO 20°	(–12° to –6°)
ZONE 9	20° TO 30°	(–6° to –1°)
ZONE 10	30° TO 40°	(–1° to 4°)

require a border plant that thrives in a shady area and discover that we can choose from (among scores of others) impatiens, hostas, or any of several varieties of creeping geraniums which could easily make us just as happy. In other words, hundreds of flowers and plants—and varieties of those plants—exist, and you will achieve much greater success with your gardening efforts by choosing the plants that will grow best in your climate and microclimate.

You must also think about the size and uses of your property. If you have limited space, think about planting bulbs or annuals in outdoor containers or window boxes. (See Chapter 4.) Containers and window boxes can also be a practical solution if you have active children who can't seem to refrain from running through your "cutting garden." On the other hand, if you consider your garden to be an extension of your house—an "outdoor room," so to speak, with a breakfast table and a Luytens bench —you will want to arrange your beds, borders, edges, and extraneous plants (like trees) accordingly.

It is also important to think realistically about the amount of time you wish to spend working on your garden. If you are a weekend gardener, by choice or necessity, think twice about planting a vast number of roses or a huge bed of annuals that may require more work than you are willing or able to do. Instead, look toward the sturdier perennials to satisfy your needs.

© Charles Mann

Left: This 'Johnson's Blue' geranium creates a lush and striking monochromatic border. Below: Containers planted with different varieties of geraniums create another attractive border.

© Derek Fell

DESIGNING THE GARDEN

From an aesthetic standpoint, designing a flower garden—particularly a flower garden planted especially for flower arranging —is a tricky business. Unlike herb gardens that are often designed in intricate, classical forms, or vegetable gardens that tend to be fairly straightforward affairs, flower gardens need to be planned so that they enhance the entire landscape of the yard, as well as produce the desired flowers.

You will probably decide that you need four or five small "gardens" or beds—perhaps a small cutting garden for annuals, a border or edging along the side of the house or along a path, and a larger border or bed containing a number of perennials, annuals, bulbs, and greens. You may also want to add one or two flowering trees.

Seasonal Considerations

Although summer is the "high" season for most flower gardens, you will probably want to make plans that allow you to have flowers in your garden for as many months of the year as possible. As a result, you need to plan for sequential blooming—beginning with spring bulbs and annuals like pansies, narcissus, and tulips; followed by summer perennials and annuals such as snapdragons, pyrethrum, petunias, and roses; succeeded by late-blooming autumn flowers like chrysanthemums, dahlias, and

© Derek Fell

© Charles Mann

Top: Chrysanthemums like these are excellent choices for late summer and autumn color in the garden. Bottom: Pansies provide fresh color in spring.

tiger lilies; and completed with not only evergreens, but with those special winter and early spring blooms that either emerge miraculously through the snow, like crocuses, can be grown indoors (tulips, primroses, Christmas cactus), or can be forced with the first hint of spring, like forsythia.

Your garden—whether indoors or out— should, if possible, contain flowers for every season.

Some Thoughts About Form

In any well-planned garden, considering "form" is imperative—not only the form of the garden itself, but the shapes of the various plants growing within the garden.

With regard to the overall garden, some plants should be large, some small. Plants should blend with the architecture of the landscape and the surrounding buildings and structures. They should flow naturally —and in graduated heights—as they edge a house or fence, or border a path.

In any flower bed, whether it is a border or a free-standing bed, the plants should also be positioned (planted) in graduated heights. In a border, the tall plants should be placed at the back of the border, and the low plants at the front. In a bed, the tall plants should be positioned in the center of the bed, the smaller plants at the outer edges. In both cases, additional plants drifting in between will create a unified, flowing look.

Include a variety of plant forms. Some flowers are tall, others low to the ground. Some have serrated edges, others have smooth edges. Some will bloom beautifully, then die back leaving rather unsightly greens. Others may have modest blooms, but leave behind attractive greens that fill in the garden plot and can also be useful and good-looking in an indoor arrangement. The size, shape, and lifelong look of the plants you cultivate should be carefully considered and planned.

Top: Here lamb's ears, iris, and monkshood in shades of purple and blue create an interesting monochromatic color scheme. Bottom: Lupines, geraniums, and lamb's ears combine equally well to make an analogous color scheme.

31

The Importance of Color

After you have decided on the spaces you wish to cultivate and the particular flowers you intend to plant, think about the "color" of your overall garden.

Of course, personal preference is a pivotal issue. If you happen to be a person who responds strongly to warm bright colors, you may want to concentrate on a red, orange, and yellow palette. If you adore blue, you will naturally want to plant flowers that will produce blooms in various shades of that color. Most people want blooms in virtually every color, especially for a "flower arranger's garden."

A bed of lupine hybrids adds interesting texture to the garden.

© Charles Mann

Color can be considered from the point of view of various color schemes: "monochromatic" schemes (all shades of the same color); "analogous schemes" (related colors); "contrasting schemes" (color opposites); and "polychromatic" schemes (many different colors pulled together). These terms relate to colors as they are expressed on an artist's color wheel.

Monochromatic schemes, which are the simplest, and can be very dramatic, are combinations of flowers of a single color such as red. In other words, all the flowering plants in your garden will be shades of red, although you could add a few white plants to accentuate the primary color.

Analogous schemes are related to monochromatic schemes, but include plants in the colors that are close to or adjacent to the primary color on the color wheel. For example, if red is the primary color of choice, you might also include orange, pink, and purple flowers. Again, white can be added to add sparkle to the plantings.

Contrasting schemes are those where the flowers are in colors that appear opposite each other on the artist's color wheel; for example, blue and orange, purple and yellow, and red and green. This approach is especially effective in a small bed of spring bulbs or an outdoor container of pansies or petunias.

Polychromatic schemes are obviously a mixture of all colors. The most obvious example of a polychromatic scheme is the

© Charles Mann

Pansies are an attractive choice for creating a striking polychromatic color scheme.

classic English country garden with a kaleidoscope of colorful plants and flowers. On one hand, the polychromatic scheme may be the easiest approach for the overall landscape—and is usually the scheme of choice. However, even though it appears to be a hodgepodge of color, the most successful polychromatic gardens have been thought through with great care. For example, a monochromatic edging might be planted in one place, an analagous arrangement in a freestanding container in another, with thoughtfully arranged, multicolored blooms in the cutting garden. Another way to achieve a considered polychromatic look

is to plant many colors of the same species of flower (tulips, for example) in one space, so that the garden achieves a consistency of form within the riot of color.

When thinking about color, you must also consider which colors will enhance the appearance of your property. If your house is gray, you may want to plant a thick border of Shasta daisies that will bloom throughout the summer (and year after year) behind a row of pink crocuses that will provide a bit of color in early spring. On the other hand, if your house is painted red, you will probably want to avoid pink blooms almost entirely.

GARDEN DESIGN CHECKLIST

Before you invest in even one seed or plant, be sure to think through your garden design carefully:

• Consider the practical issues of climate, sunlight, and soil quality

• Consider the "problems" your particular property presents, and select plants that will grow best in the microclimate of your landscape

• Think about the uses of your garden

• Make sure you have flowers and plants to fill spaces year-round

• Select a variety of plant sizes—large, small, and in between, and position them so that they create an integrated appearance, and remain in scale with other aspects of the property

• Select a variety of shapes

• Despite all these considerations, keep it simple in the beginning. Don't be afraid to use your instincts, and don't be afraid to make a mistake

COLOR IN THE GARDEN

Arranged by season, and then by color, the following is a list of potential flowers (annuals, perennials, bulbs, and shrubs) for the flower arranger's garden. With regard to the winter flowers, most are intended for indoor cultivation, except in the warmest climates:

Spring Flowers

Red
Anemone, Azalea, Bougainvillaea, Columbine, Coral bells, Dianthus, Easter cactus, Flowering maple, Fuchsia, Geranium, Hibiscus, Hyacinth, Iris, Japanese quince, Oriental poppy, Pansy, Peony, Primrose, Ranunculus, Rhododendron, Sweet pea

Pink
Anemone, Azalea, Bachelor's-button, Bleeding heart, Bougainvillaea, Clematis, Columbine, Coral bells, Dianthus, Easter cactus, Erica, Geranium, Hibiscus, Honeysuckle, Hyacinth, Iris, Peony, Perennial pea, Phlox, Primrose, Ranunculus, Rhododendron, Sweet pea, Tulip, Valerian

Orange
Azalea, Chinese-lantern, Clivia, Globeflower, Hibiscus, Narcissus, Pansy, Poppy, Ranunculus, Tulip

Top: Sweet pea comes in a wide variety of colors and makes a welcome addition to the spring garden. Bottom: Tulips also come in an almost infinite array of color, and are essential in the flower arranger's garden.

Top: 'Blue Giantess' veronica grow to about 2 feet (60 cm) high and add a vertical element to both the garden and arrangements. Bottom: Clematis, which comes in various varieties and colors, is a popular climbing vine.

Yellow

Acacia, Adonis, Azalea, Basket-of-gold, Buttercup, Columbine, Crocus, Forsythia, Globeflower, Golden star, Hibiscus, Honeysuckle, Hyacinth, Iris, Lady's-mantle, Marsh marigold, Narcissus, Pansy, Primrose, Ranunculus, Sweet pea, Tulip, Winter jasmine

Blue

Anemone, Bachelor's-button, Columbine, Forget-me-not, Glory-of-the-snow, Grape hyacinth, Hyacinth, Iris, Jacaranda, Jacob's ladder, Love-in-a-mist, Mountain bluet, Pansy, Periwinkle, Phlox, Primrose, Rosemary, Veronica, Virginia bluebells

Purple

Anemone, Azalea, Campanula, Clematis, Crocus, Daphne, Erica, Fuchsia, Hyacinth, Iris, Lenten rose, Lilac, Pansy, Phlox, Primrose, Rhododendron, Sweet pea, Trillium, Tulip, Valerian, Violet, Virginia bluebell, Wisteria

White

Allium, Anemone, Azalea, Bachelor's-button, Bougainvillaea, Calla lily, Candytuft, Cherokee rose, Clematis, Columbine, Crocus, Dianthus, Easter cactus, Easter lily, Erica, Fuchsia, Gardenia, Geranium, Hibiscus, Honeysuckle, Hyacinth, Iceland poppy, Iris, Irish moss, Lenten rose, Lilac, Lily-of-the-valley, Love-in-a-mist, Mock orange, Narcissus, Peony, Perennial pea, Phlox, Primrose, Rhododendron, Snow-in-summer, Star magnolia, Star-of-Bethlehem, Sweet pea, Sweet-sultan, Sweet woodruff, Trillium, Tulip, Violet, Winter honeysuckle, Wisteria

Summer Flowers

Red

Begonia, Bougainvillaea, California fuchsia, Carnation, China aster, Chrysanthemum, Clematis, Dahlia, Daylily, Fuchsia, Geranium, Gladiolus, Hibiscus, Hollyhock, Lily, Marigold, Nasturtium, Petunia, Pyrethrum, Rose, Salvia, Snapdragon, Verbena, Zinnia

Pink

Acanthus, Allium, Azalea, Baby's-breath, Begonia, Bougainvillaea, California rhododendron, Candytuft, Carnation, China aster, Chrysanthemum, Clematis, Dahlia, Delphinium, Foxglove, Fuchsia, Geranium, Gladiolus, Hibiscus, Hollyhock, Hydrangea, Larkspur, Lupine, Petunia, Phlox, Rose, Snapdragon, Statice, Verbena, Veronica, Zinnia

Orange

Azalea, Bougainvillaea, Calendula, Celosia, Chrysanthemum, Dahlia, Daylily, Gladiolus, Helium, Hollyhock, Lily, Marigold, Nasturtium, Petunia, Rose, Snapdragon, Zinnia

Yellow

Achillea, Artemisia, Azalea, Black-eyed Susan, Chrysanthemum, Coreopsis, Dahlia, Evening primrose, Gladiolus, Helenium, Helianthus, Lily, Marigold, Nasturtium, Petunia, Rose, Snapdragon, Verbena, Zinnia

Blue

Amorpha, Baptisia, Campanula, China aster, Clematis, Delphinium, Geranium, Globe thistle, Hollyhock, Hydrangea, Hyssop, Iris, Larkspur, Mountain bluet, Nepeta, Petunia, Salvia, Statice, Veronica

Top: Foxglove, in soft shades of white, pink, or lavender, provides attractive color and texture to gardens and arrangements. Bottom: Pot marigolds in warm shades of orange, yellow, gold, and creamy white add a golden hue to the garden throughout the summer and into fall.

Top: Iberian cranesbill add sparkle to the spring garden. Bottom: New England asters, or Michaelmas daisies, create banks of pink hues to sweeten the garden in early autumn.

Purple

Acanthus, Allium, Aster, Balloon flower, Bougainvillaea, California rhododendron, Candytuft, Chrysanthemum, Clematis, Dahlia, Delphinium, Foxglove, Fuchsia, Geranium, Gladiolus, Honeysuckle, Hosta, Iris, Larkspur, Lavender, Petunia, Phlox, Pyrethrum, Russian sage, Salvia, Statice, Zinnia

White

Abulia, Acanthus, Achillea, Artemisia, Azalea, Baby's-breath, Balloon flower, Begonias, Bougainvillaea, Candytuft, Carnation, China aster, Chrysanthemum, Clematis, Cape myrtle, Dahlia, Delphinium, Foxglove, Fuchsia, Geranium, Gladiolus, Hibiscus, Hollyhock, Honeysuckle, Hydrangea, Larkspur, Lily, Marigold, Nasturtium, Pearly everlasting, Petunia, Phlox, Rose, Saponaria, Scabiosa, Shasta daisy, Snapdragon, Statice, Verbena, Veronica, Yucca, Zinnia

Autumn Flowers

Red

Camellia, Chrysanthemum, Dahlia, Japanese anemone, Michaelmas daisy, New England aster, Pentas, Thanksgiving cactus

Pink

Camellia, Chrysanthemum, Dahlia, Japanese anemone, Michaelmas daisy, New England aster, Pentas, Thanksgiving cactus

Orange

Chrysanthemum, Dahlia, Tiger lily

Blue
Aster, Caryopteris, Gentian, Globe thistle, Michaelmas daisy, Monkshood, Salvia

Purple
Autumn crocus, Chrysanthemum, Dahlia, Michaelmas daisy, New England aster, Pentas, Veronica

White
Aster, Autumn snowflake, Camellia, Chrysanthemum, Clematis, Crocus, Dahlia, Great burnet, Japanese anemone, Michaelmas daisy, Pentas, Salvia, Silver fleece vine, Thanksgiving cactus, Tuberose, Yucca

Winter Flowers

Red
Amaryllis, Azalea, Begonia, Calla lily, China aster, Cyclamen, Hibiscus, Hyacinth, Impatiens, Nasturtium, Poinsettia, Primrose, Tulip

Pink
Amaryllis, Azalea, Begonia, Calla lily, Camellia, China aster, Christmas cactus, Cyclamen, Freesia, Hibiscus, Hyacinth, Impatiens, Miniature rose, Poinsettia, Tulip

Top: Desert candle, or Adam's needle, adds richness to the summer garden and grows throughout the winter in warm, dry climates. Bottom: China aster comes in a range of colors including white, pink, red, blue, and yellow, and blooms from midsummer to late fall.

Top: Celosia comes in a number of varieties and colors, including a warm orange like this 'Orange Kenpie.' Bottom: The iris also comes in a myriad of colors and cultivars. This one, known as 'Yellow Flag,' provides a fresh start to the early summer garden.

Orange
Calendula, Celosia, Impatiens, Marigold, Nasturtium, Snapdragon, Tulip

Yellow
Calendula, Calla lily, Crocus, Forsythia, Freesia, Iris, Lantana, Marigold, Narcissus, Nasturtium, Primrose, Snapdragon, Tulip, Winter hazel, Winter jasmine, Wintersweet

Blue
African violet, Anemone, Browallia, China aster, Crocus, Glory-of-the-snow, Grape hyacinth, Hyacinth, Primrose

Purple
African violet, Anemone, Crocus, Daphne, Freesia, Impatiens, Iris, Tulip

White
Amaryllis, Anemone, Azalea, Begonia, Calla lily, Camellia, China aster, Christmas cactus, Crocus, Cyclamen, Freesia, Hyacinth, Impatiens, Poinsettia, Snowdrop, Spirea, Tulip

© Charles Mann

Catnip is not only attractive, it serves a dual purpose—if you have a cat, that is.

Drawing a Garden Plan

Before you invest in plants or seeds, it is imperative that you draw out a detailed garden plan. Using a grid, measure the outlines of your overall landscape, and mark all immovable fixtures such as fences, patios, large trees, and driveway, or buildings, such as the house or garage. Also note changes in soil level that might affect plant growth and therefore require terracing, steps, or raised beds. Make sure that borders and beds are easily accessible for planting and maintenance. (A border should be only four or five feet [1.4 or 1.8 m] deep at most; a free-standing bed should be only four or five feet [1.4 or 1.8 m] across.)

Using tracing paper, experiment with different garden plans. Taking into consideration the number and kind of plants you want to grow, and the relationship of the various flower beds and border sights to the surrounding house or other architectural details like fences. Don't forget to include paths and walkways so that the crops are easily accessible as you plant the garden or harvest your flowers.

Work out the planting schemes carefully. (Again, you will probably have several beds including borders, a cutting garden, and outdoor containers.) Take into account plant size, shape, and color—as well as the sunlight, soil, and water requirements of the plants themselves. Try to plant perennials in places where they will not be jostled as they rest over the winter and place delicate plants in spots where they will be "safe" from children and pets.

Sophia's Country Garden

The garden on page 42 is a garden designed by Sophia Day for her country house on Long Island, New York. She tried to incorporate flowers and plants that she enjoys in colors she likes. Her house is located one mile (1.6 km) from an ocean beach, so the climate is relatively cool, and the soil is sandy and loamy. The temperature rarely gets frigidly cold in winter, so Sophia has been able to grow perennials successfully.

Sophia's property is surrounded by a high fence that protects her borders and beds from strong winds. A large, old oak tree graces the side yard, but prevents that part of the garden from getting sun. Half-

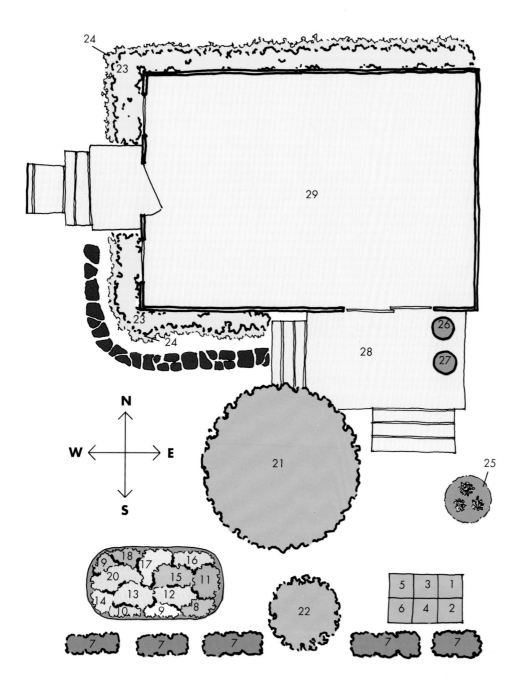

Sophia's garden

1. Oregano and marjoram
2. Rosemary and thyme
3. Tarragon and sage
4. Chives and fennel
5. Parsley and arugula
6. Various lettuces
7. Evergreen bushes
8. Dahlias (red and orange) / Tulip bulbs
9. Dahlias (white) / Narcissus bulbs
10. Rosa
11. *Philadelphus microphyllus*
12. Delphinium
13. Asters
14. *Anthemis tinctoria*
15. Coreopsis
16. Zinnias
17. Marigolds
18. Hosta
19. Nasturtiums
20. Poppies
21. Oak tree
22. Dogwood tree
23. Shasta daisies
24. Grape hyacinths and various bulbs
25. Roses
26. Potted flowers
27. Potted flowers
28. Deck
29. House

way between the oak tree and Sophia's vegetable patch, she has planted a dogwood tree, to make spring a special pleasure.

Sophia has included about 25 square feet (2.3 sq. m) for a casual cutting garden. Here, she has planted China asters, Transvaal daisies, dahlias, chrysanthemums, strawflowers, zinnias, and a few sunflowers. She chose these flowers because most of them bloomed in various shades of pink and red, colors she likes, and because many of them dry well, and she intends to dry a lot of flowers to make winter wreaths.

In a small plot next to the deck, Sophia has a "rose island" with three bushes: two grandifloras and one floribunda.

In the front of the yard, she has started modestly with an island bed that measures about 6 feet by 9 feet (2 m by 3 m), planted with some evergreens and shrubs that stay attractive-looking throughout the winter, and some greens (hosta, aureum, *Philadelphus microphyllus*) that permit the bed to look lush from spring through fall. In between, she has planted some perennials (Basket-of-gold), annuals (zinnia, nasturtium, poppies, pot marigolds), and some bulbs (tulips, freesia, and narcissus). Sophia prefers "warm" colors—reds and yellows —and has chosen to create a more or less analogous scheme with red and orange flowers interspersed with some yellow plants.

Around the deck she has planted a thick row of Shasta daisies. In front of the daisies, she has put a row of blue Browallia, which creates an attractive appearance throughout the summer.

On her deck, Sophia has placed three large wooden pots. In spring, she plants daffodils and tulips. In summer, she repots the containers with white sweet alyssum.

Purchasing Plants and Seeds

When purchasing seeds and plants, bear in mind that certain species grow better in some climates than in others. Again, check with your local garden center for those varieties that grow best in your area. (Some seed catalogues will also provide this information.)

Seeds can be purchased at garden centers, hardware stores, florists, and by mail-order. (See the mail-order sources on page 123.) Seed packets give planting instructions and are also dated for freshness, so avoid buying—or planting—outdated seeds.

Seedlings and young plants can also be purchased at garden centers, nurseries, florists, and by mail. Obviously, select only those that have green, healthy-looking foliage and appear to have been well tended. When ordered by mail, plants are usually smaller than those purchased at a nursery. Regardless of whether you order plants by mail or buy them at a local nursery, try to plant them as soon as you bring them home. If you must put off planting for a few days, keep the seedlings in a cool place, and water them regularly.

Chapter 3

CULTIVATING THE GARDEN

After the garden is planned "architecturally," the work of preparing the plants properly begins.

PREPARING THE SOIL

Preparing the soil properly is very important for the success of any garden, and particularly a flower garden. Whether you are preparing a small border, or an ambitious bed, you must prepare the soil meticulously. This is particularly true if you are planting perennials, since they will remain in the earth for years, and will be more likely to flourish if the soil is carefully prepared initially.

Preparing soil is more or less the same whether you are preparing a perennial plot, an annual plot, a place for bulbs—or a bed that will be home to a variety of plants.

In early spring, test the soil's readiness for planting by using the old-fashioned method: Pick up a handful of soil and squeeze it. If it remains in a tight ball, it is still too wet; if it feels dry and dusty, it needs to be watered deeply for several days. If it crumbles easily through your fingers, it is ready to be worked.

The first step, of course, is to mark off the areas you plan to cultivate, and then clear away existing grass, old plantings, stones, and other debris. Since you will be digging up to 8 inches (20 cm) deep, you may wish to rent a Rototiller™ for a day to help you prepare your beds.

Annuals, perennials, and bulbs all require well-drained soil. If your soil is heavy and clay-like, you will have to add organic mat-ter, coarse grit, horticultural sand, gypsum, perlite, or vermiculite to the top layer of soil. Perennials—and particularly annuals—will almost certainly require the addition of organic matter—peat moss, compost, or manure—to enrich the soil and assure proper drainage. Add the compost or other material before digging up the soil, then work it in.

The relative acidity or alkalinity of your soil—the pH factor—is an important consideration. The pH of soil is the measure of the plants' ability to absorb nutrients, and is measured on a scale of 1 to 14, 1 being the most acidic, 7 being neutral, and 14 the most alkaline. To measure the pH of soil, buy a test kit at a garden supply store or have your soil tested at a soil testing lab.

Most flowers prefer a slightly acid to neutral soil with a pH level of about 5.5 to 7. If your soil needs to be more acid, add sulfur (or additional fertilizer); if your soil needs to be more alkaline, add lime.

Flowers including bulbs require a complete fertilizer; in other words, one that contains nitrogen, phosphorous, and potassium. Fertilizer bags are clearly marked with numbers—such as 5-10-5, or some other formula that designates the proportions of the nutrients. Most flowers require a lower amount of nitrogen, since nitrogen encourages the growth of foliage and discourages flowering. Fertilize a perennial (or mixed) bed as you are preparing it. For an annual bed, fertilize as you are preparing and again later in the growing season. Soil in North America tends to be low in phosphorous, so you may need to add additional amounts of that nutrient to encourage the growth of superior blooms. Again, check with your local garden center for special needs in your area.

Once your beds are prepared, you are ready to plant your seeds or plants.

PLANTING

Annuals, perennials, and bulbs all have a variety of planting requirements, depending upon the plant and your climate. Most perennials are purchased as plants, and, for the beginner, it is probably easier to purchase annuals as plants as well. However, for the serious gardener, the purist, or the more adventuresome, both perennials and annuals can be started from seed. Some seeds can be sown directly into the garden, others need to be started indoors and then replanted.

Propagating Perennials
Perennials can be propagated in three ways: from seeds, by division, or from cuttings. Some plants do not grow quickly or easily from seed, while others, especially hybrids, produce inferior plants if grown from seeds. In either case, propagating with stem cuttings or by division is a more efficient

and effective way of reproducing plants.

To reproduce from cuttings, take the cuttings from plants in midsummer when the growth is at its height. Select a stem that has at least six leaves and cut it just above a leaf node. Carefully remove the bottom two or three leaves and any flowers or flower buds, and place the cutting in a small pot or flat in a moistened soilless medium, the same type used for growing from seed. Make sure the cutting is inserted deep enough so that the exposed nodes are covered with the medium. Cover with a clear plastic bag and place it in a warm place under bright light. After three weeks, test to see if the cutting has rooted by gently tugging at the stem. If it has rooted, remove the covering; if not, replace the bag and check in a week. Once the herb has rooted, transplant it to the garden.

To propagate by "division" is a relatively simple process. Most perennial herbs need to be divided every year or two to simulate growth. Divide herbs in spring when growth starts or in early autumn about six weeks before the first frost.

To divide, dig up the plant. Wash the soil from the roots, then carefully pull the roots apart with your hands, and replant the divisions before the roots dry out. If you divide plants in autumn, cut the plants back by half to compensate for the lost roots. Water the divisions well after replanting, then water them daily for about a week. In spring continue watering until new growth starts.

Courtesy of Gardener's Supply

Many plants can be started indoors in flats from seeds or cuttings.

Starting Seeds Indoors

Plants with delicate seeds or those that require a long growing season must be started indoors. Most annuals (as well as certain biennials and perennials that are grown as annuals) should be started from seeds six to eight weeks before they are put outdoors in the garden.

To grow seeds indoors, use flats or small pots, 2½ to 4 inches (6 to 10 cm) deep with drainage holes. Flats and containers can be used from year to year, but must be rinsed extremely thoroughly after each use. Delicate plants that do not transplant very easily should be started in peat pots so their roots will be only mildly disturbed when they are eventually moved outdoors.

Fill the flats or pots with a soilless medium made up of 50 percent peat moss and 50 percent perlite or vermiculite. Avoid using soil or old medium to start seeds since they may be contaminated with disease or old seeds. A sowing medium should always be sterile. Fill the containers to within ¼ inch (6 mm) of the top, moisten the medium, and sow the seeds according to seed packet directions. Cover the flats or pots with clear plastic or glass, and set them in a warm, well-lighted spot.

Once the seeds have germinated, remove the plastic bag or glass and move containers into full sun or place them under fluorescent "grow" lights for 12 to 14 hours per day. Water the plants from the bottom as the medium dries out, and fertilize the seedlings after they have sprouted about a half-dozen leaves. If you are using flats, transplant seedlings into individual pots when you fertilize.

Before planting the seedlings in the garden, you will need to "harden off" the plants, a process that prepares them for their new life in the outdoors. For one week before transplanting, move the plants to a protected spot outdoors for several hours every day and bring them back in at night. Each day, increase the length of time they remain outdoors. Seedlings can also be hardened off in a cold frame, which is a bottomless box set in the ground with a removable transparent top. You can buy a cold frame at your local garden center, or make one from wood and an old storm window. For step-by-step instructions, consult a basic gardening guide.

Starting Seeds Outdoors

Some annual seeds can be sown directly into the garden. Sow tender annuals only after all danger of frost has passed; sow half-hardy or hardy annuals in early spring depending upon your zone and whether or not they can tolerate frost. Sow biennial and perennial seeds anytime from spring through midsummer, or according to the specific requirements of the plant or your environment.

Before sowing seeds, water the prepared seed bed. Some gardeners scatter seeds, but usually it is best to sew seeds in neat rows and label them. Keep soil moist until the seeds have germinated. When plants are 1 to 2 inches (2.5 to 5 cm) high, thin them to the spacing recommended for the particular plant.

Planting Bulbs

Plant bulbs as soon as you purchase them or receive them in the mail. As a rule of thumb, bulbs should be planted at a depth of three times their diameter, although you should check each individual bulb for special requirements. If you are planting many bulbs close together, dig up the entire area; if you are planting them farther apart, dig a small hole with a trowel and plant each bulb separately. Cover bulbs with soil and press the soil gently.

If you are planting bulbs in a border or bed that will include annual flowers, mark the location of the bulbs so that they are not

Courtesy of Gardener's Supply

inadvertently disturbed. (Bulbs are often planted in "layers" or adjacent to perennials and annuals. Spring bulbs like crocuses will bloom in April, then several weeks later the annuals will begin to flower.) To create a country garden "field" impression in your yard, scatter the bulbs at random and plant them where they fall.

General Notes About Planting

Rules for planting apply both to store-bought plants and to those you have cultivated yourself from seed. Try to plant store-bought or mail-ordered plants immediately, but if you are unable to put them in

the ground right away, place them in pots or flats in partial shade and check them daily to be sure they are receiving enough water and light.

Plant tender annuals in mid-spring after any danger of frost has passed; plant half-hardy plants two to four weeks before the last spring frost; and plant hardy plants one to two months before the last frost. Plant biennials and perennials grown as annuals as early in spring as possible.

Biennials and perennials can be planted almost anytime, but always put them in the ground at least four weeks before the first autumn frost.

Plants tend to be "shocked" when they are first put into the ground so try to plant in the late afternoon or on a cloudy day to ease the trauma. Remove the plants from their containers carefully, so as not to disturb the root ball. If plants are in peat pots, peel away as much of the pot as possible and cover the lip of the pot with soil once it is placed in the earth. Water the new plantings daily for about one week or until new growth appears, then water once a week.

CARING FOR FLOWER BEDS

Flower beds do not require an inordinate amount of care, but some thought and consideration should be given to the basics of feeding (fertilizing), watering, mulching, and weeding. Anyone who loves gardening will almost by nature be regularly inspecting the "fruits" of their labors, and as a result will quickly observe unsightly weeds, scraggly plants, dead leaves, or the potential of disease.

With regard to fertilizing, different plants have different needs. Fertilize the bed when you prepare it, of course. Then check the requirements of specific plants so that subsequent "feeding" can be regulated properly. With perennials, fertilize each year in spring when plants first begin to show signs of life. Plants that require additional fertilizer will need feeding toward the end of the growing season. For flowers, use a fertilizer high in phosphorous. If flowering plants begin to show excess foliage and few flower buds, stop fertilizing.

Water the garden regularly. Try to moisten the ground deeply to encourage root growth and avoid watering the leaves, if possible. (A long, deep watering does more good than frequent light sprays.) New plants often require daily watering—and certainly daily watering is suggested during the heat of summer or during dry spells. For plants that like dry soil, allow the soil to dry out before watering again; for plants that like extra-moist conditions, keep the soil moist at all times. Try to water plants in the morning so that leaves will dry in the sun. (Leaves left wet overnight are susceptible to disease.)

Weeds steal light, water, and nutrients from your plants. In addition, they often carry diseases and insects. Some plants even create their own "weeds" by dropping seeds. It is important to keep the garden weed-free by picking flowers before they turn to seed, and pulling all other weeds the moment they appear.

Mulch is a protective covering that is spread over the soil and around the bases of plants to keep the ground cool and moist, to prevent weeds from sprouting, and to give the garden a finished look. Organic mulches usually consist of bark chips, leaves, hay, pine boughs, and compost, while man-made mulch can be made with black or clear plastic and newspapers. Again, the kind of mulch you select depends upon personal preference as well as the particular plants you are cultivating and their needs. If you are using an organic mulch, apply about 3 inches (7.5 cm), then leave it down to decompose into the soil in winter. (Obviously, this is not possible with plastic mulch.)

Removing dead blossoms (deadheading) encourages new growth; removing a small amount of the plant's growing tip (pinching) encourages branching and helps perennials to produce more flowers. Removing smaller side buds to make a central bud produce a larger flower (disbudding) is also something to consider. In addition, just removing spent flowers, leaves, and stalks is essential, both for the look of the garden and to preserve nutrients.

A Word About Garden Pests and Diseases

Because disease, insects, and other pests are so common in the garden, it is useful to become familiar with some of the more common ones and know some of the ways to get rid of them. Flowers, due to their fragrance and flavor, tend to ward off many insects and diseases; yet, for the same reasons readily attract other pests.

Like all garden plants, flowers may be susceptible to fungi and bacteria that produce leaf spots, wilts, and root rot. Viruses transmitted by aphids and other pests may result in mottled leaves and stunted plant growth. Insects like aphids, leaf hoppers, white flies, spider mites, beetles, and caterpillars may also attack plants and destroy leaves and roots. Other pests like grubs, maggot roundworms, snails, and slugs may also feed on flowers—slugs being particularly problematic.

In general, to avoid pests and diseases, check leaves and stems frequently for off-color or stunted tissue. Always prepare soil properly before planting seeds or plants and, if necessary, spray plants with water to dislodge insects, other garden pests, and potentially disease-ridden dust and dirt. Allow plants to dry off before nightfall, and make sure air circulates freely around leaves.

You may wish to use an insecticide or a fungicide for particular problems. Recommended pesticides vary from region to region, so check with your garden center regarding appropriate use in your area.

Slugs are one of the more prevalent garden pests. Check your plants frequently in order to avoid losing them to pests or diseases.

© Derek Fell

WINTERIZING THE GARDEN

In the fall, carefully clear your garden of all dead matter and debris, and throw undiseased plant material into the compost pile. Mulch any perennial flowers that will be living over the winter.

Fantasizing about creating new beds or adding plants to the existing garden is half the fun of gardening. Keep a notebook over the winter. Plan to experiment with new plants, and eliminate plants that did not grow well, and you will have a garden that stays beautiful and exciting indefinitely.

Chapter 4

GROWING FLOWERS IN CONTAINERS AND WINDOW BOXES

© Derek Fell

Container-grown plants can be used creatively.

Many people, especially apartment dwellers, simply do not have a plot of ground to create an outdoor garden; others do not have the time to grow and maintain a full-blown flower garden. Others want to experiment with certain flowers, or simply for the sake of appearance or decoration, want to grow certain flowers in containers or window boxes. Also, some plants, particularly perennials, can be grown in containers and moved indoors, creating "ready-made" arrangements.

As with any garden, it is important to select the right variety for special planting. Seed suppliers often specify which plants will grow well in containers as well as provide appropriate planning and maintenance instructions. Here are a few examples of plants that grow exceptionally well in pots:

ANNUALS TO GROW IN POTS OR HANGING BASKETS

Impatiens	*Impatiens wallerana*
Monkey flower	*Mimulus*
Cupflower	*Nierembergia*
Geranium (many varieties)	*Pelargonium*
Common garden petunia	*Petunia* x *hybrida*
Nasturtium	*Tropaeolum majus*
Annual phlox	*Phlox drummondii*
Verbena	*Verbena* x *hybrida*
Pansy	*Viola* x *wittrockiana*

BULBS TO GROW IN CONTAINERS

Crocus	*Crocus*
Cyclamen	*Cyclamen*
Tulips	*Tulips*
Narcissus	*Narcissus*

CHOOSING CONTAINERS

Select a pot that is in proportion to the size of the mature plant you desire to grow—or conversely, select a plant that is appropriate to the container. In addition, consider where the container will be placed. Pay special attention to sunlight (at least 6 hours per day) and wind conditions, especially if the plants will be positioned in a potentially windy spot.

Containers come in infinite shapes and materials. Plastic pots are inexpensive and easy to maintain; unglazed clay pots are more attractive but require more attention since water evaporates from them more easily. Larger, more dramatic containers require special attention since they can become quite heavy and cumbersome when they are filled with soil. (They should be put in position before the flowers are potted.)

Consider using unusual containers for potting flowers. For example, olive oil cans, oriental tea caddies, odd porcelain pieces, tea pots or sugar bowls, or even deep trays make attractive containers. Think creatively; some object you have considered tossing out may be ideal.

CULTIVATING FLOWERS IN OUTDOOR CONTAINERS

Regardless of your choice of container, all pots need appropriate drainage holes and a layer of gravel, perlite, or broken pottery to prevent water from collecting. For smaller containers, use a soilless mixture of peat moss combined with perlite, vermiculite, or coarse sand. For larger containers, mix garden soil with perlite or vermiculite.

Plants in containers need more frequent watering than those grown in the ground. Check the soil daily, especially if it is unusually hot or the plants are situated on a windy balcony or terrace, and bear in mind the needs of the particular plant. For flowers that like dry soil, water only when the soil is very dry; for those that like moist soil, water the moment the surface of the soil is dry. Potted plants may also need more fertilizer than garden plants, but be

A large, dramatic container planted with impatiens or lobelia can create a stunning focal point in the garden.

© Charles Mann

careful not to over-fertilize. Pinch leaves often to encourage growth, and if plants grow unevenly, rotate the container so that they receive light on all sides. Move the plant indoors if there is danger of frost.

Repot plants to a larger container as soon as they show signs of outgrowing their present surroundings, such as if roots begin to appear above the soil level. However, since most potted flowers are annuals, this probably won't be a problem. As with garden plants, spring is usually the best time to repot.

FLOWERS IN HANGING BASKETS

Many flowers grow well in hanging baskets which, like other containers, can be used decoratively indoors and out. In addition, some flowers that may not be appropriate for cutting—impatiens, for example—make beautiful displays in baskets and serve the purpose of a cut flower arrangement.

Plants can be potted into hanging baskets in the same way they are potted into any container. (Many plants are sold in hanging baskets.) Hanging baskets, like other containers, may need special attention. Some need to be watered more frequently, while others may require more sun or be vulnerable to wind if they are hanging outdoors.

GROWING FLOWERS IN WINDOW BOXES

A window box can be an ideal place to cultivate a miniature flower garden. If you choose to grow both annuals and perennials, separate them and pot them separately. Place the various smaller pots side-by-side in the larger window box.

A window box should be designed with the same consideration as an outdoor gar-

Window boxes, like miniature gardens, can be designed with classic form or wild abandon.

den or garden border. With regard to form, it can be formal (with single, well-organized flowers such as several rows of daffodils or two or three miniature evergreens) or it can be casual with a splash of various flowers. Color is also important. A window box can be effective in a monochromatic display of pink and white geraniums and petunias, or a polychromatic display of pansies.

Like all containers, many varieties of window boxes are available from inexpensive, lightweight plastic ones (though they tend to crack in cold weather), to clay (which also may crack), to wood. Wood-frame window boxes, although sometimes heavy, are often the most attractive and long-wearing.

before they will bloom. This is achieved by keeping them cool and dark for eight to ten weeks. (You can also buy "prepared" bulbs, but they are expensive.) Buy bulbs in early autumn and plant them immediately. Bulbs that grow well indoors include crocuses, hyacinths, daffodils, lilies, and tulips. Buy several varieties so that you can replace those that don't come up.

Pot plants to be grown indoors in the same way you pot them for outdoor containers. (See page 54.) Pay special attention to proper drainage, and consider setting potted flowers in a gravel-lined tray as an effective way to ensure sufficient drainage.

As with any potted flower, indoor flowers require special care, particularly

GROWING FLOWERS INDOORS

Although most flowers are sun-loving, many do grow well when cultivated indoors. Many annuals and perennials can be grown indoors in large containers or indoor window boxes, and make interesting floral displays. Flowering bulbs also make spectacular arrangements. Most bulbs can be grown in conventional pots, unconventional containers (like an old soup tureen), and even indoor window boxes. When bulbs are grown indoors they must experience an artificial dormancy period

© Derek Fell

Growing bulbs such as this marvelous arrangement of amaryllis, iris, cyclamen, and paperwhite can provide gardening pleasure throughout the winter. Potted plants can be used as centerpieces.

56

Courtesy of Plow and Hearth

with regard to watering, lighting, and fertilizing. Pots dry out quickly, and should be watered, both top and bottom, frequently—every day in hot weather. In addition to direct watering, sufficient moisture in the atmosphere is also important.

Light is as important as water, and special fluorescent lights are available if sunlight is insufficient. Ideally, try to use sunlight during the day and augment with artificial light if necessary. Indoor flowers also need to be fertilized every three or four weeks in spring and summer, and about every six weeks during dormant months. There are many effective and easy-to-use liquid fertilizers available for use with indoor plants. Follow the manufacturer's recommendations carefully.

Part II

DISPLAYING FLOWERS

Chapter 5

THE BASICS OF FLOWER ARRANGING

What exactly is a flower arrangement? Is it a vast urn of flowers decorating the altar of a cathedral at a dramatic wedding? Is it a meticulously arranged grouping of spring blooms adorning the table of a society matron's dining table? Is it a small collection of freshly picked daisies in a modest glass jar set on a window sill just to make you happy one afternoon? Is it one beautiful rose placed in a crystal bud vase left in the guest room to welcome an old friend?

In fact it is all of the above—and more. A flower arrangement can be a garland of evergreens adorning a mantelpiece at Christmas, a potted hyacinth on the table to make Easter dinner more festive, or the grand bouquet at the entrance of the Metropolitan Museum of Art.

In past generations, the notion of flower arranging had strict rules of form and color. Although some general guidelines still apply, the more stringent rules for "good" arrangements have been relaxed, and creativity with regard to arranging flowers is at an all-time high.

GATHERING AND PREPARING FRESH FLOWERS

Just as preparing the soil is important when you are planting a garden, it is equally imperative to prepare flowers properly for arrangements to ensure that the blooms last for the longest time possible.

Harvest flowers that are just beginning to bloom. Select tulips just as the buds are opening or daisies while the centers are still hard. Try to pick flowers that have not performed their reproductive function (pollination), since flowers wither after this time. Look at the foliage as well, and select those with sturdy, healthy stems, and bright, disease-free leaves.

It is best to gather flowers in the early morning (before flower tissues have been dried by the sun) or late in the day (when their sugar content is high, and flowers can be conditioned overnight). As you gather, cut stems on the diagonal with a sharp knife rather than snipping them with standard scissors or simply pulling them up. You might also consider investing in florist scissors, which are ideal for most flowers or pruning shears for plants with woody stems. Cut a longer stem than you anticipate needing, and clip the stem at an angle so that water can be absorbed more easily. Always handle flowers by their stems.

As you gather flowers, place them in a pail of warm water immediately. Use a plastic or enamel pail (some metal pails add minerals that can be damaging to the flowers), and make sure that the pail is clean and the water is as pure as possible.

Most flowers should be gathered and put in water with their leaves intact. However, some plants like zinnias, marigolds, asters, all chrysanthemums, and dahlias—in fact, virtually any flowers with short, wispy, or fuzzy foliage—should have their leaves removed before putting them in water since their leaves will begin to decay immediately and this will quickly damage the flowers.

Conditioning Fresh Flowers

Most flowers will last longer if they are conditioned, or "hardened" (which is not the same as "hardening off"), a process which allows the flower tissues to be filled to capacity with water.

When flowers are brought indoors, recut the stems immediately under water to discourage air from forming within the stems.

Place the stems in a pan or sink full of water, and, using a sharp knife, remove one or two inches (2.5 to 5 cm) from each stem, cutting at an angle. Then quickly place the flowers in the conditioning container—a bucket filled with cool water that comes up to the necks of the flowers.

In addition to recutting, some plants need additional preparation. Flowers that contain any milky sap—Oriental poppies or zinnias, for example—"bleed" after cutting, which prevents them from absorbing water. After recutting, either singe the ends over a flame for several seconds or immerse the ends in boiling water for about 30 seconds. If stems are recut later, repeat the process. Spring bulb flowers like narcissus and tulips should be soaked in water for several hours to drain off their sap, which tends to pollute their water.

For flowers with woody stems—such as flowering tree boughs like lilacs and rhododendrons—scrape the bark away one or two inches (2.5 to 5 cm) from the bottom of the bough or stem. Then split the stem at the base up about 2 inches (5 cm) (a cross-split is most effective). Immerse the stems in boiling water for 30 seconds, then plunge them in cool water. (To protect the flowers from the hot steam, wrap them in plastic or newspaper.)

For flowers with hollow stems like dahlias, amaryllis, or delphiniums, cut the stems straight across (rather than on the diagonal), turn the stems upside down, pour water into the stems, and plug the ends with a

Conditioning flowers

Flowers with milky sap—Singeing treatment

Flowers with milky sap—Boiling treatment

Flowers with woody stems—Cross-split stems

Flowers with hollow stems

shred of cotton or floral foam. To assure that no air bubbles form, prick the stem near the flower head, then immerse the ends in boiling water and transfer them to conditioning water. Some flowers need a wire reed inserted in the stem to hold the flower upright. Insert the reed at this point.

After flowers are conditioned, recut and treat the stems as you did before conditioning. Remove all foliage that will be submerged in water in the arrangement. Although tedious, this is the best method for producing long-lasting arrangements.

Finally, make sure your vases are clean so that unnecessary bacteria does not damage your flowers. And, of course, make sure they are filled with water at all times.

Additives

You may want to include an additive in the conditioning water, which, in theory, prolongs the life of the flowers. Specifically, additives add acidity to the water to retard bacterial growth that ultimately kills the flowers. Several additives are easily available: An aspirin or ¼ teaspoon (1 ml) of citric acid per gallon (4 l) of water is an effective method; a quarter teaspoon (1 ml) of liquid bleach per gallon (4 l) of water is another. Some people add a tablespoon (15 ml) of granulated sugar (or tonic water) per gallon (4 l) of water, which gives the flowers natural sugars for nourishment, but since sugar aids bacteria growth, combine the sugar with the bleach or citric acid.

Commercial additives are available at garden centers and florists.

Nevertheless, according to Rosemary Verey, the doyenne of English flower arranging, the best formula for prolonging the life of cut flowers is a change of fresh water every day. Too often, people add so many extra nutrients to the water that they kill rather than enliven the flowers. Ms. Verey also recommends misting flowers, removing them from drafts or heated areas, cutting off dead heads, and reconditioning after a few days.

"FORCING" FLOWERS

One of the most evocative signs of spring is a vase of blooms—often forsythia, cherry blossoms, magnolia, or lilacs—that have been encouraged to blossom just a few weeks before their "time." As early as late January or early February in some areas, branches can be gathered from the garden. Choose heavily budded stems, and cut them with a sharp knife on the diagonal. Peel back the bark and split the stems up about two inches (5 cm). Remove lower twigs and buds and put stems in deep containers of water at room temperature. (The more humid the room the better.) Change the water every other day, recutting stems each time. If you wish to use additives, add sugar and bleach.

Plants for Forcing

Japanese maple	*Acer japonicum*
Mock orange	*Bumelia*
Lemon	*Citrus limon*
Dogwood	*Cornus*
Hawthorn	*Crataegus*
Flowering quince	*Cydonia speciosa*
Forsythia	*Forsythia*
Witch hazel	*Hamamelis*
Magnolia	*Magnolia*
Apple	*Malus*
Crabapple	*Malus*
Cherry	*Prunus*
Peach	*Prunus*
Plum	*Prunus*
Pussy willow	*Salix caprea*
Spirea	*Spirea*
Lilac	*Syringa*
Wisteria	*Wisteria*

Drying and Preserving Flowers

Entire books have been devoted to the art of drying and preserving flowers, but for the purposes of this guide we will discuss only the basics. Dried and preserved flowers have a special fascination and beauty of their own and allow the flower arranger additional avenues for creativity. Drying flowers also assures that you will have attractive flowers in your home every month of the year.

Pierce wiring

Clutch-pierce wiring

Taping

SELECTING PLANTS FOR DRYING

Choose flowers and greens that are to be dried with care. Any discoloration, tears, holes, or unsightly formations are exaggerated when the flowers are dried.

Gather flowers just as they are coming into full bloom. Include buds—to be dried as such—to add variety to your arrangements. Also include seed pods either before or after they have dried on the plant. So-called weeds like "Queen Anne's lace," and wild grasses, which grow rampantly along the highway are also excellent for dried flower arrangements. (Such plants are now sold at florist shops.)

Make sure that flowers and leaves are firm and fresh. Collect plants for drying at midday when the plants have already been naturally dried by the sun. Gather more than you need, since some may be lost in the preserving process.

WIRING

For flowers with weak stems, cut just an inch or two (2.5 to 5 cm) off the stem, then wire the flower head before it is dried. The head can be wired in a number of ways, depending upon the shape and "style" of the flower. Wire can be pierced through the flower center, or the fleshy part at the top of the stem. Allow enough extra wire length to comfortably shape the wire to make an artificial stem.

AIR DRYING

Air drying is the simplest method of drying —and therefore the most popular. Remove all foliage from the stems (unless you want to dry the leaves as well) and gather the flowers into a casual bunch. As a rule of thumb, the quicker the plant dries, the more likely it is to retain its color. Therefore, remove any foliage you do not wish to keep on the final flower.

Secure the bunch with a string or rubber band or elastic. (Rubber bands work best since they accommodate the movement as the plant shrinks.) Hang the bunches upside down in a dark, dry, well-ventilated space such as from a rafter in an attic, barn, or shed. Make sure the plants are arranged with enough air to circulate around each bloom and around each bunch.

Most plants will dry within seven to fourteen days, although heavier flowers and leaves may take longer.

Some flowers require special treatment. For example, hydrangeas keep their color if quickly dried near a source of hot air, such as a heater. Plants that have a delicate stem and an umbrella head, such as grasses or Queen Anne's lace, should be dried upright.

Store dried flowers in their drying position, or put them in boxes in a dry place wrapped in tissue. (Do not wrap them in plastic, which will create moisture.)

DESICCANTS

Desiccants are substances such as sand, borax, or silica gel that are used to dry flowers by drawing the moisture out of plant tissue. Silica gel is the substance favored for most flowers because it dries plants in two or three days, thus preserving the color. Borax is used like silica gel, and it is lighter and therefore preferable when drying very delicate plants. Fine sand can also be used as a desiccant, but works best with heavier flowers like peonies. (Delicate flowers would be crushed by sand, while heavy flowers tend to become distorted if dried in silica gel or borax.)

The same method is used, regardless of the medium. Wire the flower heads. Fill an airtight container (such as a plastic box used to store food) with about 1 inch (2.5 cm) of desiccant. Lay the flowers on the substance and carefully cover them until they are buried. (Sifting the desiccant through your fingers, or slowly adding it on the side is the best method.) Allow about 3 inches (7.5 cm) between each flower; never overlap. To ensure that flowers do not flatten out, mound the desiccant carefully around each bloom.

After two or three days, wiggle or tilt the container so that the desiccant falls away from the flowers. Gently touch the leaves; if they are dry, remove them by pouring out the desiccant. (Store the desiccant in a dry place for reuse.) If they are soft, rebury them and check again the following day. It is best to dry the same or similar flowers in the same receptacle so that they dry at about the same rate.

Store the dried flowers in closed, airtight containers, upright in jars, or stuck in blocks of Styrofoam™.

MICROWAVING

It has become increasingly popular to use a microwave to dry flowers and leaves. Some leaves and greens can be dried by simply placing them in the microwave oven on a piece of paper, but it is best to combine a desiccant, particularly silica gel, with the microwaving process. Anemones, pansies, roses, tulips, marigolds, and peonies all dry extremely well in the microwave oven, preserving their shape and color to an even greater degree than when dried in the desiccant alone. (Extremely fragile flowers like baby's-breath do not dry well in the microwave.)

Place plants—again, use plants of like size, shape, and texture—in the desiccant. It is usually best to predry the desiccant in the microwave for a minute or two (until the

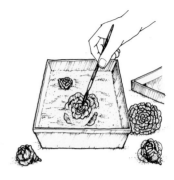

Covering flower heads with silica gel

Florist scissors

Watering can

crystals turn blue). Allow the desiccant to cool for about 20 minutes, and then place the flowers in the desiccant and dry for 2 to 3 minutes in the microwave. Experiment with one flower to get the timing down correctly and interrupt the drying every minute or so to make sure the plants are drying evenly. After they have dried, allow the plants to cool for 20 minutes before removing them from the desiccant.

GLYCERINE TREATMENT

Coarse plants, heavy leaves, and berries are best preserved with glycerine. Glycerine, available at most drug stores, works by replacing the water in the plant tissues. Although leaves treated with glycerine often change color (green foliage can turn red or deep brown), the change is generally attractive, and can work to the advantage of a creative flower arranger. Plants gathered late in the season respond best to glycerine treatment since their tissue is mature and can tolerate the change.

To preserve with glycerine, gather greens and stems, and clean them carefully. Cut the ends so that the solution can be readily drawn up. (See "Conditioning Fresh Flowers," page 61.) Make a solution of 1 part glycerine to 2 parts boiling water, and stand the greens in about 6 inches (15 cm) of the solution. Allow the greens to stand for three or four days until beads form on the leaves. (Glycerine sometimes will not be drawn into taller stems. In those cases, rub the leaves and stem ends with glycerine, or hang the branches upside down after several days.) Plants treated with glycerine can last for years and need only to be dusted or wiped occasionally with a moist cloth.

A FLOWER ARRANGER'S TOOL KIT

For a flower arranger's tool kit, you need basically the same materials you used to gather your flowers: cutting tools such as a small knife, florist's scissors, or pruning shears; a sharp knife for cutting floral foam and wire cutters for cutting heavy-gauge wire; and a thorn remover. A bottle brush for cleaning containers may also be necessary. A long-spouted water can for adding water to vases is imperative.

Vases and Containers

Of course, any arrangement requires a container. A "holder" for an arrangement may not necessarily be a traditional vase designed precisely for that purpose. Any container is a potential flower vase—and the right shape, size, color, and texture depend on the arrangement you are making. (Containers such as baskets that do not hold water will require an appropriate waterproof liner.) For more thoughts about containers, see page 54.

Mechanics: Other "Tools of the Trade"

Flower arranging is enjoying a renaissance today, and it is popular to create a more casual appearance in arrangements rather than adhering to old-fashioned, formal arranging rules. However, a knowledge of the basic tools—known professionally as "mechanics"—will help you to be more creative. All materials are available at your florist, or can be purchased through the mail. (See Mail-Order Sources, page 123.)

Pinholders—sometimes called "frogs"—are the weighted devices with pins protruding from them that are designed to hold flowers in place in a vase or container. Those made of heavy metal work best because they have more weight and are less likely to move, but pinholders are also available in lighter-weight plastic versions that are less expensive. They come in various sizes and designs, made to accommodate flowers of various sizes and weights.

Wire netting, such as chicken wire, or plastic netting, is also used to hold flowers securely. Metal netting can be wrapped around floral foam to hold the flowers, or the plastic netting can be crumpled into the container and the flowers inserted. Both can also be stretched over the top of the mouth of a container and secured with florist's tape.

Floral foam, which is sometimes referred to by its commercial name, "Oasis," is one of those products—like personal computers—that make those who use it wonder how they ever survived without it. It is a firm plastic substance, usually green, that comes in blocks or cylinders, is saturated with water, and serves to hold flowers in place. A very versatile substance that can be easily cut to fit any shape, it is also lightweight. Unfortunately, floral foam is somewhat expensive, and since it can encourage bacterial growth it should not be used more than once, unlike a pinholder.

Some foams, like polystyrene, or Styrofoam™, are designed especially for preserved and dried flowers, and treated plants.

Florist's clay is a sticky, clay substance that is usually waterproof, and is used to hold pinholders or blocks of foam in place.

Waterproof adhesive tape can also be used to hold foam in place or even to create a secure grid on a piece of foam which works like chicken or plastic wire to hold stems in place.

Floral binding tape is the flexible tape used to bind stems together in corsages or bouquets. It comes in three colors—green, brown, and white—and in varying widths.

Florist's wire is either thin or thick (it comes in varying gauges) and is used to stabilize stems in a bouquet or arrangement. It can be used for fresh or dried flowers.

Pebbles, marbles, shells, and other loose materials can be bought commercially, and when put in the bottom of a container, serve to hold flowers in place. When placed in a clear container, such elements can be decorative as well.

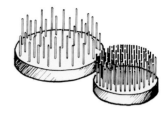

Pinholders

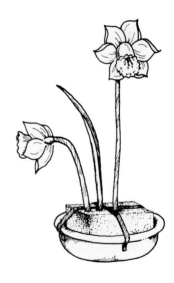

Floral foam

Chapter 6

DESIGNING WITH FLOWERS

© Derek Fell

It is not necessary to use a traditional vase for arrangements, particularly if they are informal, like this colorful group brightening up a garden bench.

The basic considerations for flower arranging apply whether you are creating a design with fresh flowers or dried flowers. In years past, certain forms were considered essential for a well-arranged formal design, and although these forms are less fashionable these days, it is helpful to have a basic knowledge of them as a frame of reference. In addition, regardless of the form of the arrangement, you must take into account the flowers you have at hand, the containers or vases you will be using, and the setting where the arrangement will be positioned.

Principles of Flower Arrangement

The general principles of flower arrangement are actually the same principles that apply to any form of design—be it painting, architecture, or sculpture: form, color, and texture.

When one speaks of the "form" of a design, one is talking about many things; overall shape, focal point, balance, proportion, and movement. In classical flower arranging, form is usually divided into three groups: line arrangements, mass arrangements, and line-mass arrangements (which, obviously, is a combination of the two).

Line Arrangements

Line arrangements are usually determined by elongated or linear plant materials such as long-stemmed flowers, spikes, or long leaves or branches, which, in turn, are used to establish the structural line. In a line arrangement, the linear materials are arranged so that they rise out of the container in an obviously vertical—or somehow startlingly visual and graceful way. Flowers and branches such as gladiolus, pussy willow, forsythia, and iris are often used in linear arrangements.

Line arrangements are often thought to be Oriental in style and origin, but in current American design they are usually considered to be contemporary. Line arrangements are usually designed to be viewed from only one angle, and will be positioned with this in mind, such as against a stark wall.

Mass Arrangements

Mass arrangements, which are European in origin, are any shape that forms a clear outline, whether it is circular, triangular, rectangular, fan, or semi-circular. The word "bouquet," literally translated, means "thicket," and a mass arrangement is a "thick bunch of flowers." Mass arrangements are intended to be more sculptural, and can therefore be viewed from all angles.

Line-Mass Arrangements

A line-mass arrangement is a combination of the two previous concepts, a form that has a strong linear element coupled with a mass arrangement often at its base. This style became popular in Europe and America in the first half of the twentieth century. (In recent years, the linear aspect was reshaped and softened into a crescent shape.) One can easily see how line-mass arrangements fit in with the Art Nouveau and later Art Deco styles of the first thirty years of this century.

General Composition

In general, flowers are combined in two ways: radial composition and parallel com-

© Derek Fell

Flower arrangements need not be confined to the indoors.

---

or tulips in a wide-mouthed, often square, rectangular, or cylindrical container.

Today, flower arranging has returned to a much more relaxed and natural look. Artists look to the ways that flowers and greens grow naturally, and try to imitate that look in an arrangement so that it never appears forced or contrived, but instead results in a flowing, natural shape.

Regardless of whether you are creating an arrangement with a classical form or a natural form, certain elements of style still remain important: focus, balance, proportion, and movement.

Focus

Any arrangement requires a central focal point, usually achieved through positioning large rounded blossoms, dramatic foliage, or even fruits at a position where the lines of the arrangement converge. Usually, focal flowers work best when positioned near the bottom of the design, since they are the heaviest. Color should also be taken into account, and the chosen focal flowers should be the brightest, or the most contrasting, or the most dramatic.

Balance

After the focal point, balance becomes the most important consideration. Obviously, in a flower arrangement, when making use of large flowers like dahlias or sunflowers, the literal balance of the vase and its contents must be taken into account. But, the

position. Radial composition is when the stems radiate out from a centerpoint, and is perhaps the most common form of arrangement, especially since flowers tend to fall in this way when pulled together in a container. Parallel composition is when stems are arranged parallel to one another. Usually arrangements of this kind are made up of one species of flower such as narcissus

arrangement must also look balanced—not top-heavy, bottom-heavy, or out-of-kilter. Even if the arrangement is intended to be asymmetrical, some effort should be made to create a counterpoint—just as in dance where the dancer will topple over when making an asymmetrical move unless he has established a gesture to balance it.

Balance can also be affected by color, particularly vivid color. For example, in a pale pastel arrangement, if you apply one vivid bloom, you must counterbalance that vivid color with a strong additional color somewhere else in the design. In fact, balance is usually best achieved by adding three similar elements, such as three spots of bright color, three larger blooms, or three sprigs of green.

Proportion
Proportion is also related to focus and balance. Flowers and greens must be in proportion to one another, as well as in proportion to the container in which they are placed. As a rule of thumb, most arrangements work best if they are one-and-one-half times the height of the container. Large bulky blooms should be placed in a more rough-hewn or heavy container; light, dainty flowers should be displayed in a delicate crystal.

Movement
In any flower arrangement, some effort must go into creating lines and masses that allow the eye to move along freely, and with pleasure. If flowers are simply stuck into a vase, the arrangement may turn out to be static and boring. If clashing colored flowers are pulled together, the arrangement becomes dissonant. Try to arrange flowers so that the eye "dances" over the arrangement, and delights in each element and in the arrangement as a whole.

Color
Color is one of the most important aspects of floral arranging, as it is in any art form. Colors seem to have certain effects on the human psyche. Warm colors—yellow and red—are usually considered happy or stimulating; cool colors—blue and green—are usually thought to be stabilizing and soothing. A bright red poinsettia adds joy to the cold winter holidays, a cool glass vase filled with airy snapdragons will make a hot summer day seem bearable.

Colors not only have an impact on human emotion, they also are capable of playing visual tricks. Warm colors (red, yellow) can jump out and seem to be closer than they actually are; cool colors tend to look receded. In the same way, color can also make the blooms appear larger or smaller than they actually are. In general, put the hotter colors up front in an arrangement and the cooler colors toward the back.

Obviously, color is very personal, but like form, some basic knowledge helps when creating flower arrangements. The rules for using color within arrangements are identical to using color when planning the garden. (See page 32.) Monochromatic, analogous, contrasting, and polychromatic schemes work the same way.

Texture

Every flower or plant has its own unique texture—thick, thin, lacy, rough, glossy, leathery, soft. In some cases, the bloom of a plant has one texture—say, velvety-soft like a rose, while its stem or leaves have another —the thorny stem and somewhat rough leaves of a rose, for example.

Texture plays a role in an arrangement, both visually and emotionally. Even if one does not touch the blooms, one can experience a tactile sense about the arrangement: Harsh colored flowers "feel" hard; soft petaled flowers are experienced as soothing.

Other Design Factors

After all the other considerations concerning the flowers and greens of a floral arrangement, one must take into consideration one last cluster of variables: the "environs." In other words, in what context are these flowers appearing? In what sort of container are they arranged? Where will that container of flowers be placed—on a small credenza, a large dining table, a windowsill? What provides the background for the arrangement—a blank wall, a mirror, a painting, a window? Finally, is this arrangement for a particular occasion—a spring

wedding, a child's birthday party, a Thanksgiving feast, or a Christmas Eve celebration? If you remember to consider these factors you will end up with a flower arrangement that is "right" in every way.

Containers

The range of containers available to the flower arranger is almost as infinite as the varieties of potential flowers. A bunch of freshly picked daffodils tied with twine and placed in a tin can might possibly project as much style and sophistication as a complex mass of spring flowers combined in a huge Steuben vase. Since the beginning of time, those containers created expressly for holding flowers—those objects we call "vases" —have been designed in virtually every substance (silver, clay, pottery, porcelain, cut glass, blown glass), constructed in virtually every size and shape, and styled by great artists from unknown Ming Dynasty artisans to Pablo Picasso. Today, we can still find man-made vases in every substance. What's more, objects not necessarily designed to hold flowers—baskets, pitchers, carafes, milk bottles, Coke bottles, and the above-mentioned tin can—are also readily available.

A flower container should enhance the flowers that it holds. It should work in proportion to the flowers, should be of a similar color or hue, or else a neutral color, so that the eye goes to the flowers, not the flower holder. In other words, as with all aspects of design—the size, shape, color, and texture of the container should complement the size, shape, color, and texture of the arrangement.

Background Considerations

The scale of a floral arrangement in its vase should be in direct proportion to the scale of the arrangement as it is positioned on a table or sill, and again, as it is arranged within the room or space. A huge arrangement positioned on a small dining table is not only visually awkward, it is not practical. A delicate, tiny display is lost in a large, open space.

The color and texture as well as the shading and light of the room also affects the appearance of the flowers and the arrangement. Multicolored flowers would clash or disappear against busy wallpaper or a colorful oriental rug. A basically dark arrangement would also disappear in a darkened room, and yet could seem warm and romantic in low light. Although light colored, monochromatic flowers against a dark background, and darker or multicolored flowers against a light background are obvious choices, an all-white arrangement in a white vase in a white room might, in fact, be spectacular. As with all aspects of design, think creatively.

Appropriate choices of flowers, containers, and general style are also to be considered. Evergreen boughs at Christmas, white roses for a wedding, and red roses at Valentine's Day are classics. However, again, creativity is imperative. What about all gold or gold and white as potential Christmas color schemes? What about pink for a Victorian Valentine bouquet? Or what about a bouquet of spring flowers in a riot of happy colors for a late March wedding? These are as appropriate as the classics—and in some ways more so, because they were chosen thoughtfully.

PUTTING IT ALL TOGETHER

Take a close look at the flowers and containers you are working with and think about the shape, texture, and colors. Prepare and condition the flowers, and prepare the container if necessary. If you are using a plain vase, you need only fill it with water. If you are filling a basket or low container, prepare floral foam by cutting it to size, securing it with adhesive clay or tape, and position wire netting over the foam if stems are relatively heavy.

Select a few important stems and create the basic outline of the arrangement—whether it is round, triangular, or semicircular. Fill in the outlined shape with flowers and greens, placing the "heaviest" at the bottom of the arrangement, and the "lightest" at the top. Position the most spectacular bloom at the center.

Chapter 7

———

A BOUQUET OF FLOWER ARRANGEMENTS

A cutting garden will yield enough vivid blooms to keep your home filled with arrangements, both fresh and dried, year-round.

© Derek Fell

The art of flower arranging is enjoying something of a renaissance in the 1990s. Throughout the world—in North America, Europe, and even the Far East—artists have rediscovered the challenges and pleasures of creating beautiful floral arrangements using classic styling techniques coupled with a modern eye. One of these artists, a young man who possesses a particularly fresh point-of-view, is Jerry Rose of Maplewood, New Jersey.

Jerry Rose literally grew up in a flower shop. His grandfather owned the first family florist business, which was originally established in Newark, New Jersey, and later moved to Maplewood. Jerry's father took over the business when Jerry was a child, and throughout his childhood and teenage years, Jerry worked in the shop. Fifteen years ago, Jerry took over management of the business, and last year opened his own shop on Maplewood Avenue.

In addition to flower arranging, Jerry has incorporated party planning and decoration into his business. Always striving for unusual and interesting effects, Jerry has applied his creative eye to developing a "total look" with flower arranging—his arrangements are not only lovely in themselves, but they also enhance the room or setting in which they are placed.

With the help of his assistant, Pam Fani, Jerry has created 22 exquisite arrangements especially for this book. Included are arrangements suitable for every season of the year, plus a number intended for special occasions ranging from a wedding to a simple autumn luncheon. Each arrangement expresses a unique and sophisticated style, yet all are easy to do, even for beginners.

LILY-OF-THE-VALLEY AND BLUE LACEFLOWER

———

This pretty blue and white arrangement is a simple paean to the flowers of spring. It is composed using just two varieties of spring flower, lily-of-the-valley and blue laceflower, both of which grow wild in some areas. When making an arrangement in a basket, it is a good idea to line it. Measure the diameter of the basket at the smallest point, and add a plastic liner of that dimension. Fill the liner with floral foam and saturate the foam with water. Then add the flowers, starting with the large blooms and filling in with the smaller ones. Use the striking lily-of-the-valley greens to give the arrangement fullness. Cover the foam with moss, such as Spanish moss, monkey moss, or any forest moss native to your area.

———

TIP: Although you have no doubt planted most of your favorite flowers in your garden, keep on the look-out for wildflowers and greens that may grow naturally in your neighborhood, in nearby wooded areas, or even, like ivy, up the side of your house. All of these can be used creatively in arrangements.

AN EARLY SPRING ARRANGEMENT

———

This "first-hint-of-spring" arrangement is perfect for an Easter dinner or a festive spring birthday luncheon. It includes purple and white columbine, blue laceflowers, grape hyacinths, and moss. The basket is made of willow branches, and the flowers are held in place by an Oasis™, or floral foam base, cut to size and soaked in water. Although the arrangement looks complex, it is really quite easy to create. Start by carefully placing the tallest blooms so that their shape echoes the contour of the basket. Fill in with the shorter blooms, balancing color and texture. Add moss to the top of the arrangement to give it a finished and natural look.

———

TIP: Color is one of the most important aspects of flower arranging. We have come to associate pastel colors with spring, probably because many flowers and greens are pale and light when they first emerge after a long winter. It's as important to take the season into account when selecting the flowers for a particular arrangement as it is to consider the color scheme, the room, or the table where the arrangement will rest.

OH, SWEET PEA

———

The delicate sweet pea is a flower not normally considered suitable for cut flower arrangements, but here it works very nicely. Instead of one container, Jerry chose to use three delicate, tall vases and one shorter, rounded vase grouped together. He selected sweet pea in four different colors—white, purple, pink, and red—then combined them with jasmine. The flowers mingle from their separate containers, creating a unified whole. (If jasmine does not grow in your climate, it can be purchased at most florist shops.) Finally, Jerry scattered tiny Limoges fruit and vegetable boxes around the flower vases to add an elegant dimension to the entire arrangement.

———

TIP: When considering containers, think about using several containers clustered together to create a small vignette. Also, many florists carry flowers and greens that may not grow well in your climate. Purchasing one dramatic flower to serve as the centerpiece of an arrangement that is filled in with flowers from your own garden can make a strong statement. Also, unusual greens can be purchased inexpensively from your local florist.

FACES OF SPRING

—

Pansies are another spring flower not normally used for cut-flower arrangements. However, here pansies have been clustered in a number of unusual containers—a toothpick holder, a sugar bowl, a creamer, and small vases of graduated heights—to create a full and dramatic arrangement. By placing several flowers of each color in every container, the disparate holders are unified under a tangle of color.

—

TIP: Consider using a planter of pansies or other potted plant as a centerpiece for an evening. Replace it on its sunny windowsill or terrace after the festivities. If you cut delicate flowers such as pansies, your arrangement will last for only one evening, but they are so lovely and hopeful-looking that they are worth the effort. Remember, pansies are thirsty flowers, so check the water in such an arrangement frequently.

SUNNY DAFFODILS

———

Simple daffodils can create a striking and sophisticated bouquet. Here, Jerry has casually grouped more than a dozen flowers in an unpretentious pottery vase, resulting in an arresting arrangement that brightens an otherwise quiet corner. In this particular arrangement, Jerry clipped the stems in graduated heights, then arranged the flowers for a lush, round effect that echoes the shape of the vase.

———

TIP: Daffodils, and other strong-stemmed flowers, can also be cut to a uniform height, and placed in a modern container such as a crystal cube, to create a sleek and modern illusion.

THE VERSATILE TULIP

Tulips are one of the most multifaceted spring flowers. They are easily cultivated, come in a rainbow of colors, and are equally attractive mixed with other blooms or arranged with great simplicity with just a few flowers of the same variety and color.

Here, Jerry has created a complex arrangement using only tulips pulled together in a clear, round vase. He has achieved an interesting diversity by combining several varieties and colors of tulips including black parrot tulips and Angelique tulips, with other more common types. To give the arrangement a sense of unity, Jerry has used at least three blooms in each color and variety. This arrangement adds drama to the somewhat monochromatic setting.

TIP: Flowers that grow from bulbs—including tulips, daffodils, and hyacinths—can be cultivated indoors in pots and then displayed in the planters as arrangements. After the flowers have emerged, just add moss to the planter to give it a "finished" look.

THE SOPHISTICATED RANUNCULUS

For some unknown reason, ranunculus is not as commonly grown or used in flower arrangements as it should be. It is quite beautiful, comes in a wide variety of colors, and mixes well with other flowers in arrangements.

Jerry chose to highlight these unusual flowers by grouping together a lush and thick cluster of unusually bright orange ranunculus. He placed them so that they seem to overflow the antique vase, and enhanced the entire arrangement by situating the vase on an antique mantel and accenting it with Staffordshire porcelain dogs.

TIP: Don't be afraid to add other elements such as porcelain bibelots, candlesticks, fruit, nuts, toys, or any favorite or appropriate object to your arrangements. Accessories can be used to enhance the beauty of the flowers.

A FORMAL BOUQUET

This formal arrangement of summer flowers is ideal for lending a sophisticated accent or focal point to a room. In an elegant white cachepot, Jerry has arranged champagne and pink roses, Queen Anne's lace, and lavender butterfly bush (Buddleia davidii). Each individual flower has a strong individual color and texture, yet they work exceedingly well together. By cutting and arranging the flowers in graduated heights, Jerry has ensured that each separate variety combines smoothly. It also gives the arrangement the height that makes it so elegant.

TIP: When creating a formal statement, don't forget to take into account the table or stand on which the arrangement will appear and the background. In this case, the dark wood background serves to highlight the elegance of the arrangement, and the bright yellow *moiré* cloth with the lace doily provides textural interest.

SWEET SCENTED STOCK

———

This lovely arrangement is ideal for a bedroom or guest room. These purple- and peach-colored stock (Matthiola incana) are known for their sweet aroma, which adds a delicate fragrance to a room. Jerry selected a metal container with a leaf motif, added a liner, filled it with floral foam, and then added the stock in a simple fan-shaped design, alternating the colors. The combination of peach and purple is unusual, yet entirely natural and therefore, effective. Lemon leaves add a welcome touch of green.

———

TIP: Don't neglect your sense of smell. Many flowers retain their scent after being picked—an arrangement that has a lovely fragrance brightens a room in more ways than one.

LOVELY LILIES

—

Lilies are among the easiest flowers to cultivate and come in hundreds of exquisite varieties and colors. Here, Jerry has created a simple yet gracious arrangement of pink Laura lilies in a tall crystal vase, and strategically placed them in front of a mirror so that the effect is doubled. His strong belief that the simpler the arrangement, the stronger the statement, certainly holds true here. This is a classic arrangement, but it has a freshness and a simplicity that is utterly modern.

—

TIP: When creating an arrangement that will sit in front of a mirror, make sure that the "back" of the arrangement is as attractive as the front since it will be reflected. Also, when using a clear container, clean stems meticulously, and change the water daily so that it is always pristine.

© Bruce McCandless

ELEGANT-BUT-EASY BRIDAL BOUQUET

This beautiful bridal bouquet was created entirely with flowers picked from the garden. Jerry combined white- and mauve-colored roses with Queen Anne's lace, white and deep purple sweet peas, and sprigs of trailing ivy. He wired them together in a tight cluster then wrapped the stems with silk ribbons in champagne and snow white. The result, a Victorian style bouquet, is perfectly romantic.

TIP: Don't be afraid to add color to a bridal bouquet or floral arrangement for a wedding party. Since white is normally associated with weddings, the base color of the arrangement should be white, but accents of deep purple, blue, yellow, pink, or champagne add richness to the pure white flowers. Ivy makes a particularly happy green to add to a wedding bouquet. It drapes gracefully and its leaves have an interesting shape.

TROMPE L'OEIL

The scene painted on this stairwell almost demanded that a real bouquet be added here! Although landings are often overlooked, they are actually ideal for flower arrangements. For this decor, Jerry created an arrangement of peach-colored spray roses accented with fresh wheat and amaranthus, which possesses the rather ghoulish popular name of "love-lies-bleeding." To soften the look of the pedestal, Jerry draped ivy around its sides. The entire arrangement echoes the painting, and the shadows it casts mingle with the painted flowers in a playful variation on the trompe l'oeil theme.

TIP: Be on the look-out for unusual places around the house to place flower arrangements: on landings or wide stairways, in bathrooms, on the kitchen table, on the front porch. Take the "fool-the-eye" concept as far as you can: Try to imitate still-life paintings that may hang on your wall; place arrangements in front of mirrors; light your arrangements creatively.

POP ART

This arrangement reflects a funkier sensibility and shows how a traditional composition can be given a modern flair. Jerry has taken formal yellow tea roses and grouped them simply in a crystal vase, but then turned the traditional arrangement on its head by combining the conservative roses with the charming frivolity of red-and-white Parrot tulips placed in three old soda pop bottles. To add to the playful effect, he has added two colorful "bathing beauty" figures. The entire arrangement, which is the centerpiece for a table, comes across as festive, clever, and amusing—perfect for a cocktail party or friendly celebration.

TIP: When creating arrangements, experiment with a variety of containers. In this case, collectible pop bottles worked perfectly. Other examples might include old perfume bottles, soup cans, children's toys, or for large flowers, an umbrella stand. Also, think about combining flowers in creative ways. Experiment with seemingly clashing colors; arrange one variety of flower in a traditional manner, then do something unusual with a second or third variety.

LILACS

Lilacs are a popular and well-loved flower. When lilac time arrives in late spring, most people cannot resist bringing an armload of the fragrant purple and white blooms into the house. Jerry has treated these lilacs in a traditional manner, creating one large, fan-shaped arrangement bursting from a big round vase that echoes the shape of the grouping. Lilac blooms so briefly that an arrangement should be lush and abundant, using both flowers and leaves.

TIP: When using tree and shrubbery branches in arrangements, be sure to condition the stems properly. Although it is wonderful to have one large, exuberant arrangement of lilacs in your house during lilac season, don't hesitate to use two or three small blooms in tiny vases and scatter them throughout the house.

Delphiniums and Dahlias

The kitchen or pantry is not generally a common spot to display flowers, but a casual, colorful arrangement in one of these rooms makes a cheerful statement. In this case, Jerry has arranged tall blue delphiniums and an assortment of orange and pink dahlias in a simple clay pot. To hold the flowers erect, he used a floral foam base in a liner. The tall delphiniums grouped within the shorter dahlias creates an ordered and striking two-tone effect that adds a spot of color and interest to the room. Next to the flower arrangement is a simple basket filled with ivy, a simple but pleasant spot of green.

TIP: Gardening tools such as simple clay pots and watering cans can make attractive containers, especially in kitchens or rooms decorated more casually. Baskets, of course, come in an infinite variety of shapes and sizes, and can be easily adapted for use as a container for flowers and greens by simply inserting a liner and filling it with floral floam. Finally, consider arrangements made only of greens, or use a houseplant as a centerpiece.

DRIED FLOWERS

—

Many flowers, especially roses, hydrangeas, chrysanthemums, dahlias, and various greens, of course, can be dried—and they can be very decorative as they dry. Here, Jerry has created a decorative yet practical arrangement along a mantel, itself an ideal place both to dry and to display flowers. The rich colors and plentiful bundles give a feeling of warmth to the setting.

—

TIP: Pick a warm, moisture-free area to dry flowers. To assure that flowers retain their color, the drying area should be dark. If possible, display flowers as you dry them using natural fibers, cord, or grosgrain ribbon to bundle the flowers together.

AUTUMN HARVEST

In a rustic wood-slated basket lined with moss, Jerry has created an unusual fall arrangement using late-summer orange spray roses, amaranthus, and orange thistles. Between the flowers he has intermingled golden corn cobs still nestled in their husks and a few Granny Smith apples. The effect is of cheerfulness and plenty, with autumn's rich colors brought indoors.

TIP: Vegetables, fruits, and nuts can make interesting additions to flower arrangements. Apples, pears, and gourds symbolize autumn and come in an infinite range of shapes and colors to blend well with fall flowers. For a more summery look, consider adding lemons, limes, avocados, or peaches.

DAHLIAS

—

Dahlias are autumn's answer to the tulip. Like their spring counterparts, dahlias come in a wide variety of colors, sizes, and shapes. They mix well with other flowers and greens or are striking when grouped simply, as with other varieties of dahlia. Versatile dahlias can be simple and homey or vibrant and elegant. This group of colorful dahlias creates a sophisticated statement when the arrangement is perched on a silver cake plate, serving as a focal point for an elegant table setting.

—

TIP: Dahlias are a must in a flower arranger's cutting garden. By late summer, they provide a profusion of color in the garden and can be displayed in virtually every room in the house.

Showy Stonecrop

—

Cockscomb, and magenta and pink sedum (also known as Showy Stonecrop) are perfect for an autumn arrangement, like this one set out for an Indian summer porch luncheon. Jerry has pulled the flowers together in an antique tin teapot that provides an interesting textural counterpoint. Sedum is one of the easiest perennial plants to grow in the garden, and its fullness and color make it work beautifully in arrangements as well.

—

> **Tip:** In the garden, select as many perennials as possible for use in flower arrangements. In addition to sedum, pincushion flowers, orange coneflowers, balloon flowers, shasta daisies, Oriental poppies, peonies, and pyrethrum all work beautifully in flower arrangements. Also, don't forget perennial "filler" plants including baby's-breath, thistles, dusty miller, and other evergreens and herbs.

Decorating for Christmas

▬

In this marvelous arrangement, Jerry has dispensed with all the floral clichés normally associated with Christmas. Instead of a traditional wreath, Jerry has arranged long stems of euphorbia (a cultivar known as 'Fire Glow') interspersed with holly and pine cones in a low basket, lined and filled with floral foam. The fullness of the greenery and bright red plumes of flowers make this an exuberant holiday arrangement.

▬

TIP: Think about your Christmas floral arrangements throughout the year. Dry flowers in appropriate colors during the summer and early autumn so that they are ready when the Christmas season arrives. For example, Euphorbia blooms in summer in northern climates, but dries well and therefore can be used in dried flower arrangements as well.

DRIED FLOWER WALL HANGING

—

Dried flower arrangements give additional pleasure because you know your arrangement will outlast a fresh one. Here, Jerry has come up with a new twist on the traditional dried arrangement—he has turned it into a wall hanging. Using flat cedar boughs as a base, he has combined hydrangea, roses, blue delphinium, and a few leaves, tying them with raffia and wire. Larger than a traditional dried-flower arrangement, this composition makes a warm wall accent.

—

TIP: Dried flower arrangements can be created in innumerable ways. For a traditional look, use baskets and pots. For a special touch, arrange flowers in an unusual pot or bowl, or a hanging basket. You can even create a decoration to hang from a door jamb, light fixture, or mantelpiece.

SUNFLOWERS

———

*Because of their size, sunflowers inevitably make a striking, eye-catching arrangement.
Here, Jerry has combined several sunflowers of different sizes. By graduating the heights
of the stems and arranging them in a tall copper pot, he has created a distinctly vertical
effect. Viburnum berries add to the rustic flavor of the arrangement.*

———

TIP: Sunflowers last into fall and combine beautifully with dahlias, zinnias, and chrysanthemums. Because they can be large, consider making dramatic arrangements using giant pots or baskets, and placing the arrangements on the floor in front of a hearth, on a wide landing, or other place that may be enhanced by a collection of large blooms.

GLOSSARY

acid: A term applied to soil with a pH content of less than 6.5.

additive: In flower arranging, the addition of a slightly acid substance to retard bacterial growth and thus prolong the life of cut flowers.

alkaline: A term applied to soil with a pH content of more than 7.3. Most herbs prefer alkaline soil.

annual: A plant that grows from seed, flowers, and then dies in one growing season.

biennial: A plant that takes two growing seasons to complete its life-cycle.

bud: A young, undeveloped flower, although it can also denote a leaf or shoot.

bulb: An underground stem or a package of fleshy scales containing stored food for the undeveloped shoots of the new plant enclosed within it; any plant that grows from a bulb such as a tulip or an onion.

compost: A blend of decomposed organic matter, which is sometimes combined with soil or sand and used to nourish plants.

conditioning: The process of preparing flowers for arranging whereby they are cut or trimmed so that water and nutrients can be drawn into them efficiently.

corm: A bulb-like stem that is modified into a mass of storage tissue.

creeping: A term used to describe a plant that trails over the ground or over other plants.

cross-pollination: The transfer of pollen from one plant to another.

cultivar: A cultivated variety of plant (as opposed to one that occurs naturally in the wild).

cutting: A leaf, bud, or part of a stem or root that is without roots. It is removed from a plant and potted to form the basis of a new plant.

deadhead: Withered flowers which should be removed to prevent seeding.

deciduous: A plant that drops its leaves at the end of the growing season; the opposite of an evergreen.

desiccants: Substances such as sand, borax, or silica gel, used to dry flowers by drawing the moisture out of the plant tissue.

disbud: To remove buds from flowers to encourage foliage growth.

division: To propagate by dividing roots or tubers into sections that are then replanted and form separate plants.

drainage: The act or method of draining water from a garden plot or container.

drying: A method of preserving herbs, seeds, and flowers by placing them in the open air for a period of days or weeks. Flowers and herbs may also be dried in a microwave oven.

evergreen: A plant that bears living foliage all year round.

floral foam: A plastic lightweight substance that usually comes in blocks, and is used to hold flowers in place in a vase or container.

forcing: The process of encouraging flowers to bloom before their natural time.

freezing: A method of preserving herbs or flowers.

genus (plural: genera): The classification of a group of closely related plants belonging to the same family.

glycerine treatment: A method of preserving coarse plants, heavy leaves, or berries using a commercial chemical product.

half-hardy: A term applied to annual plants indicating that plants so described will grow outdoors but may not survive frost.

hardy: A term applied to certain plants indicating that they will tolerate freezing conditions (annuals) or will survive a cold winter without protection (perennials).

herbaceous: A term usually applied to perennial plants whose stems are not woody and which die down at the end of each season.

horticulture: The cultivation of plants for ornamental purposes or for food.

humus: Partly or wholly decomposed vegetable matter that is used to nourish garden soil.

hybrid: A plant that results from a cross between two parent plants belonging to different species, subspecies, or genera.

invasive: A term used to describe plants that spread (often including their roots) quickly and easily from their original site.

loam: Humus-rich soil containing up to 25 percent clay and less than 50 percent sand.

mechanics: A flower arranger's term for tools such as pinholders, floral foam, and other utensils needed for flower arranging.

mulch: A covering—either organic or man-made—laid down to protect plant roots, hold moisture, control temperature, and control weeds.

peat moss: Partially decomposed moss, rich in nutrients and with high water-retention capabilities, which is often added to garden soil to add nourishment.

perlite: A substance (literally a natural volcanic glass) used to enhance soilless mediums for starting seeds and cutting, or added to garden soil to enhance drainage.

perennial: A plant that lives from year to year. The stems and leaves of a perennial die down in winter, but new shoots appear each spring.

pH scale: A system, measured on a scale of 1 to 14, devised to measure the acid/alkaline content of soil. Soils that register below 7 are acid; those above 7 are alkaline.

pinch: To remove leaves from a plant to encourage branching and growth.

pinholder: A weighted device with protruding pins designed to hold flowers in place in a vase or container.

pistil: The seed-bearing or female organ of a flower.

propagate: The process of reproducing plants.

prostrate: A term used to describe plants that lie on the ground, creep, or trail.

rootstock: The crown and root system of herbaceous perennials and shrubs. The term is also used to describe a vigorous plant onto which another plant is grafted.

runner: A stem that spreads along the soil surface, rooting wherever it comes into contact with moist soil and creating new plants.

seed: A fertilized ripened ovule that is contained in a fruit.

self-seed: A term applied to plants that drop their seeds around them from which new plants grow; self-sow.

shrub: A perennial whose stems and branches are woody and grows only a few feet high.

sow: To propagate new plants from seed.

species: A classification applied to plants within a genus.

stamen: The male, pollen-bearing part of a flower.

subshrub: A small shrub whose base (trunk) stem is woody but whose stems are soft.

thin: To weed out thickly planted growing areas, and allow plants to grow with sufficient surrounding space. Plants can be removed and thrown away, or replanted elsewhere.

till: To work the soil into small fragments where seeds or seedlings can be planted.

topiary: Evergreen trees and shrubs that have been clipped into geometric or other ornamental shapes.

tuber: A root or underground stem in which food is stored; similar to a bulb or corm.

variety: A term applied to a naturally occuring variation of a species of plant.

vermiculite: A mineral substance used together with peat moss and perlite to create a sterile soilless medium for starting seeds and cuttings.

weed: An unwanted plant in a lawn or garden. A rose bush may be considered a weed in a vegetable patch.

MAIL-ORDER SOURCES

The following are just a few of the many centers or companies across North America that supply seeds, plants, books, gardening accessories and information. Write for a catalog, or check your local Yellow Pages under "Gardening Supplies" for suppliers in your area.

Abundant Life Seed Foundation
P.O. Box 772
Port Townsend, Washington 98368

W. Atlee Burpee & Co.
300 Park Avenue
Warminster, Pennsylvania 18974
Burpee is perhaps the best-known supplier of seeds in the United States. In addition, they supply perennials, bulbs, shrubs, trees, and gardening supplies.

Brooklyn Botanic Garden
1000 Washington Avenue
Brooklyn, New York 11225

Comstock Ferre & Co.
263 Main Street
Wethersfield, Connecticut 06109
Seeds and plants for traditional garden flowers and contemporary hybrids.

Cruickshank's, Inc.
1015 Mount Pleasant Road
Toronto, Ontario, Canada M4P 2M1

Dominion Seed House
115 Guelph Street
Georgetown, Ontario, Canada 17G 4A2
They have a comprehensive catalog, but will ship only to Canadian addresses.

Gardener's Eden
P.O. Box 7307
San Francisco, California 94120
Exceptionally good-looking gardening supplies and accessories.

Gardeningport
P.O. Box 760
Thornhill, Ontario, Canada L3T 4A5

Hancock Shaker Village
P.O. Box 898
Pittsfield, Massachusetts 01202

Jackson & Perkins
1 Rose Lane
Medford, Oregon 97501
A well-known supplier of roses, bulbs, and seeds.

Moultrie Manufacturing Company
Moultrie, Georgia 31776–1179
Garden furniture, southern style: outdoor furniture, fountains, pools, sundials, birdbaths, etc.

Plants of the Southwest
930 Baca Street
Santa Fe, New Mexico 87501
Wildflowers, shrubs, and succulents suited to dry climates.

Reuter Seed Co., Inc.
320 N. Carrolton Avenue
New Orleans, Louisiana 70119
An old and respected southern seed supplier.

Roses of Yesterday and Today
802 Brown's Valley Road
Watsonville, California 95076
Old-fashioned roses and modern hybrids.

Seeds Blum
Idaho City Stage
Boise, Idaho 83706
Garden flowers and seed collections for fragrance gardens, cutting gardens, and cottage gardens.

Thompson & Morgan
P.O. Box 1308
Jackson, New Jersey 08527
The U.S. branch of a well-known British seed company. They carry a large selection of annuals and perennials.

Wayside Gardens
Hodges, North Carolina 29695
Perennials, shrubs, and wildflowers suitable for all regions.

White Flower Farm
Litchfield, Connecticut 06759
Chrysanthemums, dahlias, lilies, many perennials, ornamental shrubs.

Gilbert H. Wild and Son, Inc.
Sarcoxie, Missouri 64862
Peonies and daylilies of virtually any variety, by mail.

SUGGESTED READING

Gardening

Brookes, John. *The Garden Book.* New York: Crown Publishers, Inc., 1984.

Brookes, John. *The Indoor Garden Book.* New York: Crown Publishers, Inc., 1985.

Brookes, John. *The Small Garden.* New York: Crown Publishers, Inc., 1989.

Crockett, James Underwood. *Crockett's Victory Garden.* Boston: Little, Brown and Company, 1977.

Halpin, Anne M. *The Window Box Book.* New York: Simon & Schuster, 1989.

Halpin, Anne Moyer. *The Year-Round Flower Gardener.* New York: Summit Books, 1989.

Hobhouse, Penelope. *Garden Style.* Boston: Little, Brown and Company, 1988.

Horton, Alvin. *Arranging Cut Flowers.* San Ramon, California: Ortho Books, 1985.

Horton, Alvin, and McNair, James. *All About Bulbs.* San Ramon, California: Ortho Books, 1981.

Oster, Maggie, Consulting Editor. *Perennials For Sun.* Boston: Houghton Mifflin Company, 1989.

Packer, Jane. *Flowers For All Seasons.* New York: Fawcett Books, 1989. *This is a series of four books, one for each season of the year.*

Reilly, Ann, Consulting Editor. *Annuals.* Boston: Houghton Mifflin Company, 1989.

Turner, Kenneth. *Kenneth Turner's Flower Style.* New York: Weidenfeld & Nicolson, 1989.

Verey, Rosemary. *The Flower Arranger's Garden.* Boston: Little, Brown and Company, 1989.

Dried Flowers

Black, Penny. *The Book of Potpourri.* New York: Simon & Schuster, 1989.

Bullivant, Elizabeth. *Dried Fresh Flowers.* London: Stephen Greene Press, 1989.

Foster, Maureen. *Flower Arrangers' Encyclopedia of Preserving and Drying.* London: Blandford, 1988.

Hillier, Malcolm & Hilson, Collin. *The Book of Dried Flowers.* New York: Simon & Schuster, 1986.

Orbach, Barbara Milo. *The Scented Room.* New York: Clarkson N. Potter, 1986.

INDEX

Grateful acknowledgment is given to Anne Moyer Halpin for use of a variation of her flower color charts from her book THE YEAR-ROUND FLOWER GARDENER. © 1989 by Anne Moyer Halpin. By permission of Simon & Schuster, Inc.